HOW TO SHIT IN THE WOODS

An environmentally sound approach to a lost art

Kathleen Meyer

Ten Speed Press
BERKELEY, CALIFORNIA

Ten Speed Press
Post Office Box 7123
Berkeley, California 94707

First Printing 1989, Revised Edition 1994

Cover and text design, and typography by Fifth Street Design, Berkeley, CA
Knees by Brenton Beck, photograph by Bill Schwob
Portrait of Sir Thomas Crapper by Marilla Pivonka
Illustration page xii by Pedro Gonzalez
Chapter opening illustrations by J. S. McVey
Chapter 4 opening illustration and "Poop Tube" illustration by Jon Larson

Library of Congress Cataloging in Publication Data

Meyer, Kathleen
    How to Shit in the Woods : an environmentally sound approach
to a lost art / Kathleen Meyer — Rev. ed.
        p.   cm.
        ISBN 0-89815-627-0
        1. Mountaineering—Health Aspects—Handbooks, manuals, etc.
2. Defecation—Handbooks, manuals, etc.   I. Title.
RC1220.M6M48   1994
613'.4—dc20   94-18053
                                                    CIP

Printed in the United States of America
10 — 99 98 97

For Father,
who would have approved this subject.

In memory of Uncle Ernie,
the only other rebel and writer in the family,
who inspired and delighted me with his letters
for so many years.

And to Patrick.

Acknowledgements

Someone recently said, "This is the shortest book with the longest acknowledgments." And that it is, with the biggest bulk of contributors not even mentioned. The chapters that follow grew out of my collecting stories that generically belonged to many. What else can I say? A quick look at this list brings home for me the emotional airlift it took to become a first time author, with shit for a subject.

Untold thanks goes out to the following people: To Jon Runnestrand who always re-affirms my choosing of untrodden paths, reminding me to — above all else, in the face of disaster — keep rowing!

To Mark DuBois and Marty McDonnell who, many years ago now, gently straightened out my city ways by presenting me with a healthy dose of respect for Mother Nature and offering me the first clues as to what were the real and simple joys in life. And to Mark for his contributions and careful editing of the first edition.

To Craig Reisner for further heightening my sensitivities to human impact. To Rick Spittler for hours of environmental brainstorming.

To Howard Backer, M.D., for editing the *Giardia* section in the first edition and supplying updates for the second.

To Bruce and Suzanne Degan for their encouragement, dinners, and computer. To Michael Fahey for his special and supportive friendship, and his computer.

To my treasured women friends Carol Newman, Fredi Bloom, Martha Massey, Joanne Solberg, Jennie Shepard, Linda Cunningham, Jan Reiter, and Katya Merrell for surviving with me through all the nutziness of life's daily turmoil. And to Fredi for her inexhaustible contributions of levity. And Joanne for her ever open, sun-filled guest room and for our all-night sister gabs.

To darling Jean Hayes for the blessings of clarity and the freedom to become.

To the late Fred Bond and his wife Edith, and Ronita and Frank Egger for being my families.

To my mother, gone forever now, for believing in me and in this subject when she was ninety years old.

To Silvio Piccinotti for his wonderful old stories and generous ways and teaching me to drive draft horses; our mornings clopping down the road kept me grounded and sane through writing the original manuscript and then prepared me for the next evolution in my life.

To Susan Adams for the sweet honesty of her friendship, her unflagging encouragement, and her readings of the manuscript at many stages.

To Suzanne Lipsett, ace friend and editor, for providing honest but smiling swift kicks.

To Sal Glynn — the man who might have become a great saucier, had he not ended up a superior editor. It was a pleasure!

To Robert Stricker, my agent and dear man, for beating down my door and making everything happen and happen and happen. And to Ten Speed Press for a thoroughly enjoyable publishing experience.

To countless others who offered encouragement, direction, inspiration, instruction, or life-support. To name a few: Connie Thomas, Marilla Pivonka, Bruce Raley, Robert Volpert, Bonnie Evans, Norm Frankland, Art Schemdri, Carolyn Takher, Susan Still, Catherine Fox, Esther Young, Elizabeth Young, Stephen McDade, Lorene and Ron, Cameron Macdonald, John Suttle, Gary Ellingson, Fran Troje and Patricia Doyle.

To all those helpful persons — voices without faces — at the Environmental Protection Agency, Center for Disease Control and Prevention, U.S. Forest Service, Bureau of Land Management, National Park Service, Canada Park Service, Grand Canyon River Permit Office, numerous sanitary districts, San Anselmo Public Library, U.C. Medical Library, and Missoula's St. Patrick Hospital Library and the Maureen and Mike Mansfield Library. I mention directly only a few: Bob Abbott, LuVerne Grussing, Roger Drake, and Baird Beaudreau.

To Lenore Anderson at Colorado Outward Bound, Rich Brame at National Outdoor Leadership School, Dr. Charles Helm, Donald Studer, and Shirley Volger Meister. To Dan Ritzman for rainy days at take-outs. To all at Recreational Equipment, Inc. (REI), Marin Outdoors, and, in Missoula, The Trailhead.

To the many who have written to me (there has been no shortage of eagerness to comment on this subject), you will find much of the information incorporated in the revised edition.

And finally, of course, to everyone who so unabashedly shared a worst shit story knowing that it would be spread before the world. You know who you are; I won't mention any names.

Contents

Introduction . . . . **xiii**

Author's Note . . . . **xv**

Chapter 1 Anatomy of a Crap 1
Techniques — Style — Getting Comfortable

Chapter 2 Digging the Hole 13
Why and How and Where to Dig an Environmentally Sound
Hole — Transmission of Enteric Pathogens (Intestinal Diseases)
— Symptoms of Giardia — Cryptosporidium — Soil Types —
Locating the High Water Line — Stirring — The Latrine —
Problems of Winter and Ocean Disposal

Chapter 3 When You Can't Dig a Hole 31
Toiletry for Rock Climbers, Arctic Trekkers, Sea Kayakers —
High Use Areas — Sensitive Ecosystems — Packing It Out —
Group Shitarees — Organic Sweeteners

Chapter 4 Plight of the Solo Poop Packer 55
Becoming a Poop Packer — Containers for the Individual —
Backcountry Solar Outhouses — Beetles and Such — Frosting
a Rock

Chapter 5 Trekker's Trots 65
Diarrhea — Coping with the Unexpected — Prevention — Field
Water Disinfection — Filtration Systems — Virus Protection —
Traveler's Medical Sources — Recreational Reading

**Chapter 6 For Women Only: How Not to Pee
in Your Boots** 85
Peeing Techniques — Managing Menstruation in the Wilds —
The Feminine Funnel

Chapter 7 What? No T.P.? or Doing Without 95
Wilderness Alternatives — Eating Like a Horse

Definition of Shit 103

Afterword 107

I dyde shyte thre grete toordes.

Fables of Aesop, Caxton Translation, Vol. 15, 1484

Thou shalt have a place also without the camp, where thou shalt go forth abroad: And thou shalt have a paddle upon thy weapon: and it shall be when thou shalt ease thyself abroad, thou shalt dig therewith, and thou shalt turn back, and cover that which cometh from thee.

Deut. 22:12–13

Introduction

In response to Nature's varied calls, *How to Shit in the Woods* presents a collection of techniques (stumbled upon by myself, usually in a most graceless fashion) to assist the latest generation of backwoods enthusiasts still fumbling with their drawers. Just as important is the intention to answer a different, more desperate cry from Nature in conveying essential and explicit environmental precautions about wilderness toiletries applicable to a variety of seasons, climates, and terrains.

For many millennia our ancestors squatted successfully in the woods. You might think it would follow that everyone would know how by instinct. Nature simply takes its course when a colon is bulging or a bladder bursting. But "its course," I cheerlessly and laboriously discovered, was subject to infinite miserable destinations.

Several seasons of guiding city folks down whitewater rivers both sharpened my squatting skills and assured me I wasn't alone in the klutz department. Frequently, the strife and anxiety experienced in the bushes were greater than any sweat produced by the downstream roar of a monster, raft-eating rapid. Those summers on the river led me to a couple of firm conclusions. *One*: Monster rapids inspire a lot of squatting, which in turn supplies a wealth of study material for *two*. *Two* (and ultimately one of the subjects that prompted this publication): Finesse at shitting in the woods — or anywhere else, for that matter — is not come by instinctively. This might sound as though I were a regular Peeping Joan. But with several dozen bodies squatting behind the few bushes and boulders of a narrow river canyon, I found it practically impossible not to trip over a few — exhibiting all manner of contorted expressions and positions — every day. Generally, a city-bred adult can expect to be no more successful than a tottering one-year-old in dropping his or her pants to squat. Shitting in the woods is an acquired rather than innate skill, a skill honed only by practice, a skill all but lost to the bulk of the population along with the art of making soap, carding wool, and skinning buffalo.

We are now several generations potty-trained on indoor plumbing and accustomed to our privacy, comfort, and convenience. To a person brought up on the spiffy, silenced, flush toilet hidden away behind the bolted bathroom door, elimination in the backcountry can degenerate rapidly into a frightening physical hazard, an embarrassing mess, or, incredibly, a week-long attack of avoidance constipation.

Over the last couple of decades, an unprecedented lust for wilderness vacations and exotic treks has exploded out of our metropolitan confines. With the same furor that marked the nineteenth-century race to fulfill Manifest Destiny, rat race victims now seek respite in the wilds from twentieth-century urban madness. Masses of bodies are thundering through the forests, scurrying up mountain peaks, and flailing down rivers, leaving a wake of toilet paper and fecal matter Mother Nature cannot fathom. It's not unrealistic to fear that within a few more years the last remaining pristine places could well exhibit conditions equal to the world's worst slums. Anyone who has come upon a favorite, once-lovely beach or river bank trashed with litter knows the horror. But greater than the visual impact of rapidly increasing human waste in the woods are the veiled environmental consequences. Tragically, no longer can we drink from even the most remote, crystal clear streams without the possibility of contracting giardiasis, a disease spread through fecal deposits in or about the waterways — a disease unknown in the U.S. wilderness prior to the 1970s.

Once the "authorities" have taken over preservation, it is, in my mind, already too late. Rules and regulations imposed by government agencies (though absolutely necessary now in many areas) are themselves rude incursions into majestically primitive surroundings and antipodal to the freedom wildness represents. Rules, signs, application forms, and their ensuing costs are truly a pain in the ass, brought about not solely by increased numbers of persons, but also by the innocently unaware and the blatantly irresponsible. The willingness to inspire preservation comes most naturally from those who delight in the wilds; it is they — we — who have the greatest responsibility for respect, care, and education. And it is we who must learn and teach others how and where to shit in the woods.

Author's Note

For several years, *How to Shit in the Woods* lay dormant, a collection of scattered ideas on scraps of lined yellow paper tucked in a drawer, while I grappled with a seemingly insurmountable problem: terminology. How was I to refer to this *stuff* that is pushed and squirted out of the body in response to eating and drinking?

Since the days of Adam men have been announcing that they were going off to take a piss, leak, dump, or crap. Although references to the subject do not abound in history, conjecture would have Eve and her female descendants declaring the same until those allegedly delicate of heart, weak-stomached Victorian ladies began fainting at the sound of such language. Daintiness and propriety contracted an allergy to the foregoing diction that is considered odious to this day. Yet someday, I suspect, cultural fashion will dictate another sweeping back-to-basics movement and relieve this parlance, currently deemed macho, of its inelegance.

Loathing most things fashionable and having at one time worked with street kids, I confess that my own language can quite easily become delightfully raw and debased. I salute macho (in this instance) in the interest of directness. Still, I was reluctant to begin by offending most readers, education — not alienation — being the goal in mind. The process by which I resolved this semantic difficulty is worth sharing.

In everyday speech around everyday friends, I admit I'm partial to the words *shit* and *pee*. Running through all the alternatives produced no sound solutions. Studding an entire book with *urination*, *defecation*, *elimination*, and *stools* seemed depressingly clinical. The pronunciation alone of the terms *bowel movement* or *BM* seems to emit something foul — from my childhood, I remember them being breathed in whispers. *Bathroom* and *restroom* are euphemisms not applicable in the woods; even *outhouse* and *Porta Potti* do not fit where they do not exist. *Scats*, *turds*, *dung*, *chips*, *pellets*, and *pies* are useful mainly in zoology and dirty jokes. *Constitutional* seems overly prissy in addition to being misleading, since I never heard of anything but a "morning" constitutional, easily confused with a brisk turn in the fresh air. *John, johnny, head, potty, wee-wee, pee-pee, whizz, Number One* and *Number Two, tinkle, poop, load, poo-poo, doo-doo, ca-ca,* and "going to see a man about a horse" — all a little indirect or too cutesy.

Next, I tried circumventing the problem by relying on description and avoiding particular terms altogether. But the prose became lengthy and cumbersome; plus, I was certain I'd be accused of not calling a crap a crap. There I was, stuck again, and not another noun in sight.

My mind slowly began wandering back over the tangle of verbiage looking for a new trail, something missed. I remembered my father had always purported to be within his genteel rights in using the word *piss* because Shakespeare had employed it. Father's strategy seemed excellent (though he was technically wrong; it was Jonathan Swift), and over the years my refined (verging on priggish) mother did grow, if reluctantly, to accept this argument. Though she never came to use the word herself, in time the wince that wrinkled up her face upon its utterance became almost indiscernible. Thus, with a solid case in point and mother's brief but significant evolution in mind, a defensible logic began to take hold.

The printed word has a way of inventing truths (as the success of several sleazy national tabloids attests) and of influencing acceptable usage, with *Webster's* dictionary being considered the most reliable reference. A great excitement seized me as I noted that although my 1957 unabridged edition of *Webster's* contained no mention of *shit*, the library's 1988 edition did include the term plus a three-line definition. Aha! what do you know? Linguistic history in the making.

Next, I remembered something E. B. White wrote about language that stuck in my mind, no doubt, because of his choice of metaphor — rivers being close to my heart:

> *The language is perpetually in flux: It is a living stream, shifting, changing, receiving new strength from a thousand tributaries, losing old forms in the backwaters of time.*

Shit hadn't been lost in any backwater. White might well be horrified by my using his explanation for my justifications, but, unwittingly and to my great joy, I found he supplied more and more defense for my crystallizing rationale:

> A new word is always up for survival. Many do survive. Others grow stale and disappear. Most are, at least in their infancy, more appropriate to conversation than to composition.

By no means had *shit* grown stale. For hundreds of years *shit* had survived with ease. I knew it to be an old word: I'd seen it written as *scitian* in Old English, as *shyte* in Middle English. Currently, *shit* abounds in daily conversation. But since *Webster's* is still proclaiming its usage as "vulgar," I concluded the word was lolling in its infancy.

With the needed precedent set in 1988, I fell right into keeping with father's old strategy. My lacking the literary stature of Shakespeare or Jonathan Swift became no matter. Feeling as exuberant as one of E. B. White's thousand burbling tributaries, I proposed to help wash this great word, *shit*, downstream to its confluence with greater maturity and on into the ocean of acceptable usage. There it might float around in the company of all other words deemed proper for composition. And so it was that I comfortably settled on the promotion of *shit* (and *pee* along with it) accompanied by splashes of the clinical and cutesy in appropriate places.

Shit is a superb word, really. Sometimes *shit* can be music to my ears. It doesn't have to be spoken in hushed, moralizing tones. SHIT! OH, SHEEIT! A versatile, articulate, and colorful word, it is indeed a pleasure to shout, to roll along one's tongue. A perfectly audible — if not ear-shattering — remarkably ordinary, decent, modest everyday word.

Furthermore, it is my thought that in legitimately defining *shit*, I might engender some small credibility for the word with anyone still shocked by its usage. *Pee* seems unnecessary to define here, since according to the *Oxford English Dictionary* it is already a euphemism for *piss*. It is also a familiar and cultured sound: we have Ps and peas and appease.

For the too well-bred then and the overly delicate, for the betterment of the English language, and perhaps for the next edition of *Webster's*, I offer (it is for the reader to decide whether shamelessly) at the end of the text a complete, unabridged definition of *shit*. For all its subtleties of meaning, this word is extremely unambiguous. *Shit*, in fact, is one of the least misunderstood words in use today.

As I'm winding up the second edition of *How to Shit in the Woods*, it occurs to me it may be some few centuries before the word *shit* loses its firecracker appeal to children. I relate the following story:

> Once upon a time, a woman friend of mine, a farrier by profession, sat on her commode reading a few pages of my book — in fact, the very pages preceding this one. Rolling over in her mind my theories on the evolution of the word *shit*, she came upon the notion of imparting to her children a new attitude toward the sound of s-h-i-t. Their generation might then, she thought, grow up in plain acceptance of the word, reacting to it as they might now to puppy or bubble gum. At that moment, her seven-year-old son appeared at the bathroom door asking if she would accompany him to the trampoline. On impulse she said, "Just as soon as mama's through shitting."
>
> SHITTING? MAMA'S SHITTING? His eyes bulged, growing round as his trampoline. Out to the yard he ran, broadcasting to his brother and inadvertently the whole neighborhood: MAMA'S SHITTING!!!

◆

With Victorian nastiness barnacled to the word and act of shitting, we might all do better to think of the subject in its Oriental acculturation, wherein human *night deposits* are used to replenish the richness robbed from the soil in the growing of crops. Shit — oh, glorious shit — makes all life possible. This is so! If we stop doing it, we die. If we stop doing it — Mother Earth dies.

Possibly we could coordinate my farrier friend's effort at advancing etymology by synchronizing a time around the globe to tell all seven-year-olds about shitting. Then we can all be aghast together while our offspring shout to the neighbors. The whole thing should be over in a week.

ANATOMY
OF A CRAP

*Bowels are not exactly a polite subject for
conversation, but they are certainly a
common problem. . . . Please think of me
again as the urologist's daughter. . . . It may
disgust you that I have brought it up at all,
but who knows? Life has some problems
which are basic for all of us — and about
which we have a natural reticence.*

Katharine Hepburn, *The Making of The African Queen*

I n the mid-1800s in the Royal Borough of Chelsea, London,
an industrious young English plumber named Thomas
Crapper grabbed Progress in his pipe wrench and with a number of sophisticated sanitation inventions leapfrogged ahead
one hundred years. T. J. Crapper found himself challenged by
problems we wrestle with yet today; water quality and water
conservation. Faced with London's diminishing reservoirs
drained almost dry by the valve leakage and "continuous flush
systems" of early water closets, Crapper developed the *water
waste preventer* — the very siphonic cistern with uphill flow
and automatic shut-off found in modern toilet tanks. T. Crapper & Co Ld, Sanitary Engineers, Marlboro Works, Chelsea
(as his name still appears on three manhole covers in West-
minster Abbey) was also responsible for laying hundreds of

T.J. Crapper and his wonderful invention.

miles of London's connecting sewers — and none too soon. The River Thames carried such quantities of rotting turds that the effluvium had driven Parliament to convene in the early morning hours to avoid a vile off-river breeze.

For the Victorian ladies who complained of the WC's hissing and gurgling as giving away their elaborately disguised trips to the loo, Crapper installed the first silencers. Such pretenses as "pricking the plum pudding" or "picking the daisies" were foiled when a lady's absence was accompanied by crashing waterfalls and echoing burbles. Among Mr. Crapper's other claims to fame were his pear-shaped toilet seat (the forerunner of the gap-front seat) designed for men, and the posthumous addition to the English language of a vibrant new word: *Crapper!*

Clearly, T. J. Crapper was ahead of his day. Progress and time, nonetheless, are peculiar concepts. Some things in the universe — pollution, the use of euphemisms, *sneaking* off to the bathroom and tinkling silently down the side of the bowl, to name a few — seem to defy change, even from century to century. But there's been one glaring reversal in regard to crap. Our advanced 1990s populace, well removed from the novelties and quirks of the first indoor WCs, finds itself having to break entirely new ground, as it were, when relieving itself outside. Ironically, shitting in the woods successfully — that is, without adverse environmental, psychological, or physical consequences — might be deemed genuine progress today. Take Henry, for instance (a namesake, perhaps, or even a descendant of old King Henry VIII).

All the stories you are about to read are true (for the most part), having been extracted from dear friends and voluble strangers on various occasions, sometimes following the ingestion of copious quantities of Jose Cuervo or Yukon Jack. Only the names have been changed to protect the incommodious.

High on a dusty escarpment jutting skyward from camp, a man named Henry, having scrambled up there and squeezed in behind what appeared to be the ideal bush for camouflage, began lowering himself precariously into a deep knee bend. Far below, just out of their bedrolls, three fellow river runners violated the profound quiet of canyon's first light by poking about the commissary, cracking eggs, snapping twigs, and sloshing out the coffee pot. Through the branches, our pretzel man on the hill observed the breakfast preparations while proceeding with his own morning mission. To the earth it finally fell, round and firm, this sturdy turd. With a bit more encouragement from gravity, it rolled slowly out from between Henry's big boots, threaded its way through the spindly trunks of the "ideal" bush, and then truly taking on a mind of its own, leaped into the air like a downhill skier out at the gate.

You can see the dust trail of a fast-moving pickup mushrooming off a dirt road long after you've lost sight of the truck. Henry watched, wide-eyed and helpless, as a similar if smaller cloud billowed up defiantly below him, and the actual item became obscured from view. Zigging and zagging, it caromed off rough spots in the terrain. Madly it bumped and tumbled and dropped, as though making its run through a giant pinball machine. Gaining momentum, gathering its own little avalanche, round and down it spun like a buried back tire spraying up sand. All too fast it raced down the steep slope — until it became locked into that deadly slow motion common to the fleeting seconds just preceding all imminent, unalterable disasters. With one last bounce, one final effort at heavenward orbit, this unruly goof ball (followed by an arcing tail of debris) landed in a terminal thud and a rain of pebbly clatter not six inches from the bare foot of the woman measuring out coffee.

With his dignity thus unraveled along sixty yards of descent, Henry in all likelihood might have come home from his first river trip firmly resolved to never again set foot past the end of the asphalt. Of course, left to his own devices and with any determination at all unless he was a total fumble-bum, Henry would have learned how to shit in the woods. Eventually. The refining of his skills by trial and error and the acquiring of grace, poise, and self-confidence — not to mention muscle development and balance — would probably have taken him about as long as it did me: years.

I don't think Henry would mind our taking a closer look at his calamity. Henry can teach us a lot, and not all by poor example. Indeed, he started out on the right track by getting far enough away from camp to ensure his privacy. Straight up just wasn't the best choice of direction. Next he chose a location with a view, although whether he took time to appreciate it is unknown. Usually I recommend a wide reaching view, a landscape rolling away to distant mountain peaks and broad expanses of wild sky. But a close-in setting near a lichen-covered rock, a single wildflower, or even dried up weeds and monotonous talus when quietly studied, can offer inspiration of a different brand.

The more time you spend in the wild, the easier it will be to reconnoiter an inspiring view. A friend of mine calls her morning exercise the Advanced Wilderness Appreciation Walk. As she strides along an irrigation canal practically devoid of vegetation, but overgrown with crumpled beer cans, has-been appliances, and rusted auto parts, she finds the morning's joy in the colors of the sunrise and the backlighting of a lone thistle.

Essential for the outdoor neophyte is a breathtaking view. These opportunities for glorious moments alone in the presence of grandeur should be soaked up. They are soul-replenishing and mind-expanding. The ideal occasion for communing with nature is while you're peacefully sitting still — yes, shitting in the woods. The rest of the day, unless you're trekking solo, can quickly become cluttered with social or organizational distractions.

But back to Henry, whose only major mistake was failing to dig a hole. It's something to think about: a small hole preventing the complete destruction of an ego. A proper hole is of great importance, not only in averting disasters such as Henry's, but in preventing the spread of disease and facilitating rapid decomposition. Chapter Two in its entirety is devoted to *the hole*.

More do's and don'ts for preserving mental and physical health while shitting in the woods will become apparent as we look in on Charles. He has his own notion about clothes and pooping in the wilderness: he takes them off. Needless to say, this man hikes well away from camp and any connecting trails to a place where he feels secure about completely removing his britches and relaxing for a spell. Finding an ant-free log, he digs his hole on the opposite side from the view, sits down, scoots to the back of the log, and floats into the rhapsody that pine tops find in the clouds. Remember this one. This is by far the dreamiest, most relaxing set up for shitting in the woods. A smooth, breadloaf-shaped rock (or even your backpack in a pinch in vacant wasteland) can be used in the same manner — for hanging your buns over the back.

This seems like an appropriate spot to share a helpful technique imparted to me one day by another friend: "Shit first, dig later." In puzzlement, I turned to her and as our eyes met she watched mine grow into harvest moons. But of course, "shit first, dig later" — that way you could never miss the hole. It was the perfect solution! Perfect, that is, for anyone with bad aim. Me? Not me.

Unlike Charles, there's my longtime friend Elizabeth who prizes the usefulness of her clothes. While on a rattletrap bus trip through northern Mexico, the lumbering vehicle on which she rode came to a five-minute halt to compensate for the lack of a toilet on board. Like a colorful parachute descending from the desert skies, Lizzie's voluminous skirts billowed to the earth, and she squatted down inside her own private outhouse.

Occasionally it is impossible to obtain an optimal degree of privacy. Some years back, my colleague Henrietta Alice was hitchhiking on the Autobahn in Germany, where the terrain was board flat and barren. At last, unable to contain herself, she asked the driver to stop and she struck out across a field toward a knoll topped by a lone bush. There, hidden by the branches and feeling safe from the eyes of traffic, she squatted and swung up the back of her skirt, securing it as a cape over her head. But Henrietta's rejoicing ended abruptly. Out of nowhere came a column of Boy Guides (the rear guard?) marching past her bare derrière.

There are many theories on clothes and shitting, all individual and personal. In time you will develop your own. Edwin, our next case study, has a new theory about clothes after one memorable hunting trip; whether it be to take them off or keep them on, I haven't figured out.

For the better part of a nippy fall morning, Edwin had been slinking through whole mountain ranges of gnarly underbush in pursuit of an elusive six-pointer. Relentlessly trudging along with no luck, he finally became discouraged, a cold drizzle adding to his gloom. Then a lovely meadow opened before him and its beauty caused him to pause. His attention averted from the deer, he now relaxed into a gaze of pleasure, and soon became aware of his physical discomforts: every weary muscle, every labored joint, every minuscule bramble scratch — and then another pressing matter.

Coming upon a log beneath a spreading tree, Edwin propped up his rifle, quickly slipped off his poncho, and slid the suspenders from his shoulders. Whistling now, he sat and shat. But when he turned to bid it farewell, not a thing was there. Oh, hell! In total disbelief, Edwin peered over the log once more, still finding nothing. The sky opened and it began to rain and a pleasant vision of camp beckoned. Preparing to leave, he yanked on his poncho and hefted his gun. To warm his ears, he pulled up his hood. There it was! On the top of his head, melting in the rain like a scoop of ice cream left in the sun.

Poor Edwin will not soon forget this day; he walked seven miles before coming across enough water to get cleaned up. Though I fear he was in no humor to be thinking much beyond himself, we can only hope he did not wash directly in the stream. To keep pollutants from entering the waterways, it's important to use a bucket to haul wash water well above the high water line of spring runoff. But I digress, and this topic is covered thoroughly in the next chapter. For now, back to techniques.

At eighty-six years old, my dear Uncle Ernie cautioned old people fearful of toppling over while squatting (old people?) to steady themselves by holding onto a branch or tree trunk. My theory is to find a place to sit: I'm really Charles, the sitting dreamer, in disguise.

If you are a good squatter and also in a hurry, perhaps to chase a caribou or click off pictures of the sunset, you might try a technique perfected by one of our elected U.S. officials. We'll call him Jonathan the Deer Hunter, and, I might add, the Ham. His is a rare performance, an adagio of fluid motion and perfect balance. One night after midnight at the tail end of a venison barbecue bash, I mentioned I was writing this book and received a mock demonstration on the living room rug.

Sinking into a hang ten surfboard pose — knees bent and arms outstretched from the shoulder — Jonathan scrapes a trench four to five inches deep with the heel of one cowboy boot (this works only where the earth is fairly soft). Instructing those of us now left in the living room, he suggests dropping your jeans (and drops his) either to just below your hips or all the way to your ankles, pointing out that folds of material are uncomfortable when bunched up in the bend at the back of your knee. After squat-straddling the ditch for as long as it takes, he drops in his paper and shoves the excavated dirt back into the trough with the instep of his boot. In finale, he packs the dirt down the way any good gardener would finish planting a tree. It was a marvelous performance, I had to agree, except for the toilet paper in the hole — the telltale sign of humans on the planet. We'll discuss this later.

From the depths of a lumpy sleeping bag, from the middle of many a wilderness campsite, has come this sort of question, accompanied by a bit of a whine: "Herbert? Whaddo I do if I have to go in the middle of the night?" Secretly, Herbert might have an identical first-timer question himself, so I'll answer this one for him.

Unless there's a full moon or you have the nocturnal instincts of the snails that go for my petunias, carry a flashlight for those midnight jaunts. As much as I dislike anything resembling civilization in the boondocks, I will concede that in unfamiliar terrain, a tiny light bulb can prevent a stubbed toe, a cracked head — when you trip and pitch over the cliff — or, more commonly, two weeks of the itchy crotch-crazies from lurking poison oak. Many contributors to this book have confessed to one of those "I hoped I wouldn't live long enough to tell the story" stories. Poison oak seems to be the most common misadventure of night squatting.

One further caution: make it a *small* flashlight. The searchlight variety is overkill and can predispose the body to more permanent damage from irate fellow campers. There's nothing like waking up in the middle of peaceful nowhere to someone crashing through the bushes with their high beams and a roll of toilet paper.

Observant caution is always the recommended approach in selecting a place to relieve oneself. Poison oak is not the only dastardly culprit abroad. As my friend Ma Prudence Barker notes, one cannot just plop down with wild abandon in any old daisy field — especially a daisy field — and hope to escape unscathed. Ma once knew a logger named Lloyd who experienced the unequivocal misery of being nailed by a bumble bee smack on the family jewels. Logger Lloyd swore the pain was worse than any chainsaw nick, bullet hole, or careless imprint of spiked Currins Caulk tearing into flesh.

It is prudent to inspect any area for hazards where you plan to sit down bare-assed. You wouldn't want to become an outdoor casualty as did the subject of this poem by Shirley Vogler Meister.

The Ex-Camper

Though city-bred, he learned to camp
and loved to trek in dew and damp
until a creeping critter found
him crouching with his denims down.

Snakes are notorious for sleeping tucked under rocks and logs. Ants run around everywhere. And there are places in the world, as the noted writer and explorer Tom Cahill discovered, where a person can't squat without carrying a big stick to beat off the local pigs. Always check around for damage you might incur, and check for any damage you might inflict.

One morning on the Owyhee River in Oregon, our party had already broken camp, loaded the boats, and tied down everything securely. We were standing ready to push off into the current when it became apparent to me that the morning's coffee had arrived at the end of its course through my innards.

"Wait, wait," I cried to everyone and raced up the bank. I wound through the jumble of boulders until a convenient rock presented itself. Yanking down my shorts, I sat down and began watering the face of the rock.

Now the southeastern corner of Oregon is home to the chukar, a relative of the partridge. This chunky, chicken-like bird is saddled with a reputation for being absurdly stupid and has the added hereditary misfortune of a lunatic voice. A cuckoo bird with the hiccups couldn't sound sillier. Audubon calls the chukar a "hardy game bird that can outrun a hunter (first flying uphill, then flying down)." It's been more my experience that if you decide upon a chukar for dinner, you could walk right up to one, hand it a stone, and it would agreeably hit itself over the head for you. Combine the bird's inability for anything resembling graceful flight with its darting, quickstepping motion reminiscent of an old-time movie, add long hours spent ridiculously burping its own name, and the chukar becomes cause for much amusement.

Still propped on the rock, I was appreciating a final glance around one of my favorite river camps while enjoying the pleasure of a shrinking bladder. Suddenly there came a loud, crazed *chuk-karr chuk-karr*. A great flapping motion arose from between my knees, convulsed into my face, and then vanished. I knelt down before the wet rock. Tucked beneath a small overhang, behind a clump of grass, I found a precious woven nest holding eight warm eggs — now lakefront property on the edge of a puddle of piss. In one great swoop of karma, all my abusive snickering and pompous guffawing, my enjoyment at the expense of this poor species of fowl, had come home to roost and I felt terrible. Atop a nearby boulder after her fit of apoplexy, the ruffled mother sat staring at me. While heading back to the beach, I chided the powers that be for not giving me a more acute sense of smell or hearing — in the absence of experience — and resolved to do more vigorous battle with my ignorance.

◆

Most of the foregoing stories are worst-case scenarios. I have recounted them not to scare you out of the woods, but to acknowledge the real perils and suggest how to work around them. Life itself is a risk; you could trip headlong over your own big toe or swallow your breakfast down the wrong pipe any day of the week. And have you *ever* tried to locate a toilet downtown — a task fraught with more frustration than any possible misfortune outdoors? Someone (not me) really needs to produce instructions for how to shit in the city.

I'll just say this: Disasters of elimination in the city can be more excruciatingly humiliating than those in the bush. Sometimes I think storekeepers, clerks, and tellers all must be terribly regular, "going" at home in the morning and then not needing a *terlit* (as my grandmother from Brooklyn would have said) for the rest of the day. If there *is* a stinking, grime-coated john tucked away in the far reaches of a musty storeroom, for some reason this information is as heavily guarded as the most clandestine revolutionary plans. In tramping around town, I've all too often encountered locked doors, scribbled *Out of Order* signs, *Employees Only* plaques, or "I'm sorry we don't have one" fibs. Sometimes, the only recourse is to streak for home and hope to get there in time. I'll take the backcountry, thanks.

So, get on out there. Find a place of privacy, a "place of easement" as the Elizabethans knew it. Find a panoramic view — one that can't be had with a Liberty quarter and the half turn of a stainless steel handle. Go for it!

DIGGING
THE HOLE

Landscape is sacramental, to be read as text.

Seamus Heaney, *Preoccupations*

When we try to pick something by itself, we find it hitched to everything else in the universe.

John Muir, *Daily Journal*, 1869

Now for the serious stuff. People — corporate lawyers, philandering spouses, presidential candidates — always want to know how to bury their shit. This chapter spells out precisely where and how to dig holes that promote rapid decomposition of feces and prevent contamination of waterways, thereby providing the best protection for the health of humans, the remainder of the animal kingdom, and the planet. Before we can hope to fathom how great is the importance of properly digging our own small *one-sit hole* (also termed *cat hole*) in the bush, it's necessary to try to envision our shit in the global sense. *Try* is the trick here.

Exactly where does the world's collective excrement go? Not a pleasant question. How often do any of us think about where it goes after it's sucked down the hole at the bottom of the bowl? Possibly never. Such reflections tend to detour our consciousness, barring those rare occasions when we have to call Roto-Rooter.

Approached from any angle, the actual physical dimensions of this pile of yuck produced upon our globe befuddle imagining. Nevertheless, let's go back to the Mesozoic era and try thinking across the ages — across mountain ranges, across continents — to the present. Let's begin with dinosaur scats.

In all probability, the *Stegosaurus* and *Tyrannosaurus rex* let rip with something roughly the size of a Cadillac. The piles left by the woolly tusked mammoth might have been somewhat smaller, say TR3-sized — nonetheless a formidable turd. To the total of the dinosaurs' leavings add the excrement of Cro-Magnon man (and woman) and the wandering tribes. Add the feces of polar bears, black bears, brown bears, gorillas, hippos, and giraffes. Add buffalo chips. Add tiger and rhino dung. Total up the dumps of the Romans (remembering their gluttonous ways), the Vikings (that stout-of-digestion breed), and modern man, woman, and infant (by all means, infant — we know how the human baby goes at it). Include the scats of elephant and lion, deer and antelope, moose and kangaroo, caribou and wallaby. Toss in every species that birdshits — from pterodactyl to parakeet. And finally round up the output of hogs, dogs, horses, cows, rabbits, owls, cats, and rats. And in imagining all this, you've put a mere chicken scratch on the surface.

Anyone who's been responsible for the maintenance of a cat's litter box understands how turds have an inherent tendency to pile up like junk mail. And anyone who has skipped across a cow pasture has spent at least a few seconds marveling at the size of those rippled pies (if not sailing the dried ones for Frisbees). Now, multiply one — just one — litter box or cow by 230 million years. Gadzooks!

Since the minutest scrap of life began wriggling around on our planet, Mother Earth has valiantly been embracing fecal waste in an astounding display of her natural absorption capacities. An infinitely bottomless garbage pit, however, does not exist. There are times when the amount of waste becomes far too great for it to be amassed comfortably against her bosom. And the amount of the waste can often have less to do with the problem than the manner in which it's discarded.

Take, for instance, all the campers in a national park on one good-weather weekend and imagine them as a herd of buffalo corralled in a space the size of your backyard. Or take a boatload of refugees, rolling and tossing, seasick on ocean swells, and visualize them locked for two months inside your favorite movie theater without plumbing. In the absence of properly functioning or adequately dug disposal facilities, accumulated fecal matter rapidly grows into a major sanitation problem, sometimes with devastating consequences. Under such conditions, diseases find king-sized footholds from which to run rampant. Epidemics — not to mention assaults on the aesthetics — are common in regions where the tonnage of yuck exceeds absorption capacities. Fecally transmitted diseases are endemic in most developing countries, but they are not unheard of in the United States.

Until roughly fifteen years ago, no one ever considered it unsafe to drink directly from mountain streams. You could stretch out on the bank of a high mountain meadow creek and just push your face into the water to drink. In 1977, the Sierra Club backpacker's guide still touted drinking directly from wilderness waterways as one of the "very special pleasures" of backcountry travel. In 1968 Edward Abbey wrote the following in *Desert Solitaire* (new edition, New York: Ballantine, 1985):

> *When late in the afternoon I finally stumbled —*
> *sun-dazed, blear-eyed, parched as an old bacon rind*
> *— upon that blue stream which flows like a miraculous mirage down the floor of the canyon, I was too*
> *exhausted to pause and drink soberly from the bank.*
> *Dreamily, deliriously, I waded into the waist-deep*
> *water and fell on my face. Like a sponge I soaked up*
> *moisture through every pore, letting the current bear*
> *me along beneath a canopy of overhanging willow*
> *trees. I had no fear of drowning in the water —*
> *I intended to drink it all.*

But no longer can we *drink it all* — no longer can we drink even a drop before purifying it without running the risk of getting sick. According to the Federal Center for Disease Control and Prevention in Atlanta, no surface water in the world is guaranteed free of the microscopic cysts responsible for a parasitic disease called giardiasis. This is a disease not easily eradicated, either in the wilds or in the human body. Though not fatal in healthy adults, it can be an unpleasant and debilitating illness and, in some cases, chronic. For the young, the old, or the frail, it can be worse. It is also possible to have the disease, show no symptoms but, nonetheless, be a carrier. Giardiasis is a relatively new disease in the medical community and the general public can be instrumental in promoting an awareness of it. To that end, I've reprinted here a list of specific symptoms:

Symptoms of Giardiasis (commonly called *Giardia*)

1. A large volume of foul-smelling, loose (but not watery) stools seven to ten days after ingestion, accompanied by abdominal distention, flatulence, and cramping, especially in conjunction with wilderness or foreign travel (other sources to consider are domestic dogs and cats and preschool daycare centers).

2. Sudden onset of explosive diarrhea seven to ten days after ingestion.

3. Nausea, vomiting, lack of appetite, headache, and low-grade fever.

4. Acute symptoms can last seven to twenty-one days and may become chronically persistent or relapsing.

5. In chronic cases, significant weight loss can occur due to malabsorption.

6. In chronic cases, bulky, loose, foul-smelling stools may persist or recur — they may float and be light in color.

7. Chronic symptoms may include flatulence, bloating, constipation, and upper abdominal cramps.

8. Many individuals, unknowingly, are asymptomatic passers of cysts.

[If you think you have Giardia, *you should see a physician for stool testing and have medication prescribed, though it's thought that most cases resolve spontaneously within four to six weeks. With any diarrhea illness replenishing body fluids is critical. Keep in mind that the symptoms given above are nonspecific; many other problems can exhibit the same symptoms. In fact, when testing stool samples nowadays, it is recommended to test for both* Giardia *and another protozoan prolific in surface waters,* Cryptosporidium, *discussed later in this chapter.]*

◆

The actual spread of the *Giardia lamblia* parasite into the backcountry is an interesting and as yet incomplete story. Though the particulars of transmission are still under study, it has been determined that strains can be passed between animals and humans. Like many of the world's enteric pathogens (intestinal bugs), *Giardia* is spread by "fecal-oral" transmission, meaning some form of the infectious organism is shed in feces and enters a new host or victim by way of the mouth. The *Giardia lamblia* protozoan has a two-stage life cycle. The active stage, the trophozoite, feeds and reproduces in the intestine of the animal host; any *live* trophozoites excreted in feces die off rapidly. The second stage, the dormant cyst, which is also passed in fecal matter, is much hardier and able to survive in an outside environment.

Direct fecal-oral transmission of *Giardia* cysts is a concern in preschool day care centers and other institutions. This type of transmission by direct person-to-person contact (and also transmission via contaminated food) can easily be eliminated in the outback with careful attention to hand washing. It is the waterborne transmission that poses a bigger problem in the wilds. Once the cysts have entered lakes and streams, they can remain viable for months — particularly in cold waters.

Giardia cysts have been discovered in mountain headwaters, the alpine feeders that spring to life from rainfall and eventually wash down to form all our watercourses. Concentrations are higher in some rivers and streams than in others; studies show that both occurrence and concentrations change regionally and seasonally. It is still possible to scoop a cupful of pure water directly from a stream, but the risks aren't worth it. Technically, as soon as water falls from the sky and lands on the ground or bubbles to the surface from a natural spring, it is possible for *Giardia* to be present. Only a few cysts need be ingested and enter our intestinal track to cause infection. In "Eat, Drink, and Be Wary" (reprinted from California Wilderness Coalition in *Headwaters*, Friends of the River, March/April 1984), Thomas Suk discusses various paths by which fecal material enters wilderness waterways:

> . . . *direct deposition by humans or animals into*
> *water, and deposition near water where the cysts can*

> be carried into the water by runoff, rising water lev-
> els, erosion, or on the feet of humans or animals.
> Cysts may also be carried to water on the haircoat of
> animals who roll in feces.

Giardia is present nowadays in much of the animal kingdom, with strains having been found in fish, birds, reptiles, and
thirty mammalian species. Animal feces continue to contaminate
remote watersheds, although it is not completely clear just how
many are transferable to humans (or vice versa). Beavers and
muskrats, spending their lives in the water, are known carriers.
But the saddest commentary on this disease is that humans may
play a substantial role in spreading it around the world.

Prior to 1970, there were no reports in the United States
of waterborne outbreaks of *Giardia*. The first waterborne outbreak occurred in Aspen, Colorado, in 1970. Over the next four
years, many cases were documented in travelers returning from,
of all places, Leningrad. The explanation for this seems to be a
combination of two factors: the Soviet Union became more
open to visitation by Westerners at about this time and Leningrad's municipal water supply was full of *Giardia* cysts. The U.S.
outbreak sparked debate and speculation, as well as ongoing
research, into the origins and the manner of transmission among
species. Where did it come from? Who gave it to whom? Who
bears the greatest responsibility for its spread, animals or
humans? What do we do now?

A popular theory, seeming to exonerate humans, is that
Giardia has been around all along — throughout the eons —
and is only now being correctly diagnosed. "Around" could be
the key word in this theory. *Giardia* may have been around
somewhere, but in the Sierras? In the Rockies? Undeniably, in
other parts of the world, there have been reports of *Giardia*
since it was discovered in 1681. I can't help but recall that
numerous river cronies and I drank from watersheds all over
the western U.S. and Canada throughout the late sixties and
into the mid-seventies and never came down with *Giardia* —
other intestinal disorders on occasion, but not *Giardia*. Only in
the late seventies and early eighties did we begin to hear
repeatedly of unshakable cases of this "new disease" among us.

It seems improbable that we were all previously either asymptomatic carriers or misdiagnosed.

To further humor my personal suspicions as to where the responsibility for the spread of *Giardia* lies, I offer a few more thoughts. If left *solely* to the animals in the wild, it seems the progression might have marched along at a different pace, beaver to beaver, stretching over a long period of time — hundreds, even thousands of years (perhaps never to have reached us at all owing to Darwinian selection or a build up of natural immunities). It is known that both humans and animals can and do spread this disease. There is also evidence to suggest that animals can rid themselves of *Giardia* during the winter months only to be reinfected by humans in the spring.

Until a few years ago, New Zealand's wilderness waterways, for reasons not altogether clear, were reported *Giardia*-free. It was thought due possibly to the country's strict quarantine regulations on all incoming livestock and pets, the island's inherent isolation, and/or the absence of indigenous water mammals. In 1991 we sadly learned *Giardia* reached New Zealand's pristine shores. The following year, at opposite ends of the earth, another *Giardia*-free pocket succumbed: Nahanni National Park — a remote area (access by fly-in only) in Canada's Northwest Territories.

Another parasite with the impressive name *Crytosporidium* (causing the illness cryptosporidiosis) is now being found in backcountry surface waters and, according to one study, with more frequency and in higher concentrations than *Giardia*. *Cryptosporidium* may sound familiar to you; it made headlines in 1993 as the cause of a waterborne outbreak in Milwaukee that affected in the neighborhood of 400,000 people. As a protozoan, it is similar to *Giardia* in all the following ways: fecal-oral transmission, intestinal propagation, viability in water for long periods, passage between humans and animals, characteristics of acute symptoms, potential for chronic affliction, and occurrence of asymptomatic carriers. *Cryptosporidium*, however, is highly resistant to chlorine — much more so than *Giardia*. The estimated twenty-one million Americans who receive municipal drinking water from systems dependent on chlorination without filtration are at risk. Don't stay home merely in the hope of avoiding contaminated drinking water. For backcountry travel, there are many field water filtration systems that will eliminate protozoan parasites.

Before drinking, here is what you must do. Treat all back-country surface water — stream, lake, waterfall. Treat spring water unless it's contained in a concrete housing that provides security against contamination from surface water and animal feces. Along the Appalachian Trail you'll find a few concrete housings around springs. Keep in mind that the water is only as good as the housing; springs with old crumbling or cracked housings are suspect. Finally, treat even municipal drinking water in developing countries and when advised in the U.S. For backcountry treatment advice, see the section on field water disinfection in Chapter Four.

In the final analysis, in the continuing search to accurately determine the reasons for the spread of *Giardia* and *Cryptosporidium*, one earnest issue comes to light above all others: It is a matter of grave import for us — animals, such as we are, possessing a great mental capacity — to recognize the potential extent of our impact on the total animal kingdom. Too often we fail to take fully into account the ramifications of our fast-living, expedient ways, which reverberate through every other aspect of life on the planet — eventually boomeranging to haunt us.

In retrospect, the appearance of these parasites could be of great benefit to us, if they teach us only that we are capable of spreading odd, new diseases as fast as we take vacations. Think about it. What animal other than *Homo sapiens* can swallow *rogani gosht* in India or *Kalya e Khass* in South Africa and shit it into the Colorado countryside?

Permit me one last muse on the global subject of spreading diseases before we take up our trowels to dig holes. In most of Africa and parts of the Middle East and South America, surface waters are infested with *Schistosomes*, the blood flukes that cause schistosomiasis (also called Bilharzia after the discovering physician). The presence of these flukes precludes any swimming or wading, as their manner of entry is through the skin. Into these waters, the late great environmental activist Edward Abbey would not have dared to dip even his parched big toe to cool off. Fortunately for us in North America, one stage of a *Schistosome's* life cycle must take place in a snail found only in the tropics. But then again, who out there can promise me that at some future date, a minor mutation in the blood fluke's thermostat might not leave this parasite completely compatible with our temperate zone, garden variety escargot? Highly unlikely — but if not Bilharzia, then something else is bound to arrive upon our shores (probably already has).

The best line of defense for protecting our wild lands, our wild friends, and ourselves is to develop scrupulous habits of disposal — dig an environmentally sound hole and bury that shit — and a compulsion for educating newcomers to the woods with a similar fastidiousness.

◆

Now, pick up your backpacker's trowel or old army-entrenching tool and prepare to dig. For those lacking a proper tool, the *U-dig-it* ($20 – $25 from U-dig-it, 3953 Brookside Lane, Boise, ID 83703, 208-939-8656), is a palm-sized stainless steel trowel with a folding handle and a belt sheath. You can plant trees with this instrument and never torque it into the useless half gainer I've made out of numerous cheaper models. It's been tested in military survival schools and is guaranteed not to bend or rust for five years.

Choosing a good excavation site for the one-sit hole requires some knowledge and preparation. The objective in digging a hole is to inhibit the passing of disease-causing organisms by humans or animals or storm runoff into nearby surface waters and by flying insects back to food areas.

There is no one best set of rules for all terrains, seasons, and climates. In fact, such a collection of variables and trade-offs exists that at first it might seem one would need four PhDs to sort them all out. For example, the decomposition rate of buried fecal material is greatly influenced by all of the following: soil types and textures, filterability (as measured in percolation rates), moisture content, slope of terrain, general exposure, insect inhabitation, pH, and temperature.

The trade-offs in environmental protection are between security and decomposition. The ideal spot for rapid decomposition (*rapid* is completely relative here; under the best conditions, human shit can take more than a year to vanish) is dry to somewhat moist, but not excessively moist, with abundant humus and bacteria. To better understand this description, think of the perfect place as being shaded by vegetation or even a rock formation

— but not in a drainage area affected by storm runoff or at a site intermittently inundated by an annual rise in water table.

Feces deposited in extremely parched soils in open locations may not be at much risk of removal by runoff. But this kind of ground is difficult to dig into, and the lack of bacterial activity in the meager topsoil could mean that deposits take nigh on forever to decompose. In areas above timberline or in sub-zero climates, bacterial activity in the soil is virtually nonexistent. It is better to pack your poop out — no kidding! — or at least back to where it can be buried in good earth. In highly limited conditions there is a further option: *frosting*. Procedures for *packing-it-out* and *frosting* are covered in Chapter Three.

If you are interested in becoming a burying expert or boggling your mind further with all these variables, Harry Reeves has written a fascinating article, "Human Waste Disposal in the Sierran Wilderness" (*Wilderness Impact Studies*. San Francisco: Sierra Club Outing Committee), reporting the findings of an extensive field study. For the rest of us, one twentieth-century philosopher has stated it well, "One can do *only* what one can do," and so it is with the search for the ideal hole. Our goal, therefore, will be to dig holes that are as ecologically sound and aesthetically pleasing as our layman's knowledge and the rest of this chapter will allow.

The primary consideration in choosing a burial site is to prevent feces from becoming washed into any waterway. Even when buried, the bacteria in human waste is capable of traveling a good distance through the surrounding soil. Choose a location well away from creeks, streams, and lakes — 150 feet is generally recommended, though I find this figure is difficult to apply to anything other than lakes. (Reservoirs with highly fluctuating water levels are not, as most are named, lakes.) Canyons carved by flowing waterways have vastly different configurations. You can walk away from one for three miles and still remain in the flood plain, while with another you may need to climb two stories to find a secure spot.

The best plan is to stay above — well above — the high water line of spring runoff. This line is not always easy to locate. In some terrain, the high water line can be as elusive as the other sock — the one you swear went *into* the drier. With a bit of training, you'll be able to find it.

The great gush of springtime water created by snowmelt usually brings down a load of debris: gravel, rocks, boulders, brush, limbs, even tree trunks. Invariably, as the flood waters peak, slow, and drop, portions of this debris become beached on open shores or caught in riparian vegetation, settling in a relatively horizontal line. In steep river canyons, as you float along on a late season water level, this line may be stories above your head. You might look skyward in mid-river and notice a huge tree trunk deposited curiously atop a house-sized boulder, so high and dry by midsummer you'd guess only giants could have placed it there.

Another clue to the high water line is a watermark — a bathtub ring — left as a horizontal stain on a canyon's rock walls. Some watercourses rage only in the spring or during flash floods from thunderstorms and are bone dry the remainder of the year. Learn to develop an eye for terrain and drainages — the low spots, the canyon bottoms, the erosion gullies, the dry washes. Ask knowledgeable locals to acquaint you with how high a river rises during its spring runoff. Gradually, you'll learn to estimate the level fairly accurately from the shape and steepness of a canyon. When in doubt, climb higher; next year might be the cyclical big one — the twenty-five-year flood.

Winter landscapes require more skill on our part. Spring's high water line is obliterated under drifts of snow. Terrain is difficult to determine, and the chances of squatting on top of a buried stream bed increase when you are not familiar with an area from previous summer visits. Steer clear of flat, open places, as they may be frozen ponds or wide meadows, the latter being a mountain's flood plains that gather and funnel water into creeks. The best advice is to head for high ground. In deep snowpack or sub-zero temperatures, when you can't dig into the frozen earth or sometimes even dig far enough to find earth, the recommendation again is to pack-it-out.

The next and most thankful thing to learn about digging is that you're not required to dig to China. Quite the contrary: the most effective enzymes for breaking down excrement live within the top eight inches of the soil. It's generally recommended that you dig down six to eight inches. This allows sufficient coverage of dirt to discourage animal contact and to keep flying insects from vectoring pathogens back to food areas.

Stirring is a brilliant new technique that we all need to learn and employ. It is that "mixing" of the item we've deposited in our *one-sit hole* with loose dirt scraped from the sides of the hole before covering it over, all to the purpose of enhancing the decomposition rate by way of bringing soil bacteria in contact with a greater portion of the turd. Use a small stick for this purpose, something you can drop into the hole, not a tool you will be returning to your belt-sheath or backpack. Think ahead. Pick up a downed stick along the way to your mission site, and when first digging the hole, loosen some dirt from the sides. Where there are no sticks, be creative. Use a stone. Carry a few Popsicle sticks you don't mind parting with. Be aware that "no sticks" may mean a high use area, an area with no bacteria in the soil, or an area with no soil — situations, once again, where *packing-it-out* is environmentally preferable to burying it.

The merits of stirring come to us as far back as 1982 in a study conducted in Montana's Bridger Range ("Potential Health Hazard from Human Wastes in Wilderness" by Kenneth L. Temple, Anne K. Camper, and Robert C. Lucas, *Journal of Soil and Water Conservation*, November–December 1982, Volume 37, Number 6). Fecal matter inoculated with bacterial pathogens *E. coli* and *Salmonella* was buried in cat holes. *Salmonella* proved a hardy survivor at all sites over the winter; *E. coli* persisted at some. Researchers theorized that fecal matter may actually insulate bacteria from the breakdown action of soil and proposed that mixing soil and feces might speed up die-off. No one could imagine backcountry recreationists employing such a practice. Now here we are . . . stirring!

A trekker's urine is an altogether different story. Pee evaporates rapidly and is relatively sterile, unless some sort of bladder infection is present (and a sufferer is usually aware of such a condition). The major cautions with peeing are to keep away from high use areas where the stench becomes unpleasant and to avoid peeing on rocks and gravel where urine will leave a lasting odor. In certain areas, notably Grand Canyon beaches, the National Park Service instructs people to pee directly into the river or on the wet sand at the water's edge. The pee is washed away by the daily fluctuations in water level created by Glen Canyon Dam upstream. These procedures were not adopted solely to eliminate rank urine smells; the concentration of pee (containing nitrogen) that boaters would otherwise deposit upon the soils of the Grand Canyon — an arid and slow-changing environment — would rapidly alter the soil chemistry. The volume of river water in the Colorado, upwards of 15,000 cubic feet per second, also warrants this practice. Over the course of a year, that amounts to about one part pee to about fifty-five million parts water. Or as calculated by National Park Service district manager Mark Law, the equivalent of twenty-eight thousand cases of beer. Follow this procedure, however, only when the park or forest service specifically requests it.

For *any* type of eliminating, you should first wander a good distance from a camp area, not only for privacy, but to avoid squatting on potential sleeping spots or kitchen sites. If you are moving your camp every day, use this to advantage by making deposits in the areas of least visitation along your route. This is called elimination "on the move." Stay away from trails, which are in themselves high use areas. Plan ahead, or you will find yourself skipping off the trail to the first available nook — one which doubtless had the same appeal to many before you. Certain regions are predictably deep in shit, such as the shores just upstream of hellbender rapids. (Nothing can get bowels moving faster than thinking you're going to die.)

Let's focus for a moment on the subject of toilet paper. I recently met an ex-rock climber who related the following story. While clinging to a ledge halfway up Yosemite's Half Dome, the urge suddenly came upon her. Rock climbing is the least regulated of outback activities, and rock climbers are notorious for just letting it fly, bombs away! It's not uncommon to hear stories of climbers who've been hit on the head. But in this instance, the climb was organized to be respectful of the mountain and other climbers. Remaining safely in her leg loops, she skillfully peeled down her pants and positioned her carryout container. Next, she ripped off an arm's length of toilet tissue and then somehow let go of it and watched it quietly float away. The paper curled downward only for a moment before being snatched by an updraft. For the better part of an hour, soaring, diving, looping, happy as a mime artist, this tail of tissue entertained everyone strung across Half Dome. Need I say more about hanging onto your t.p.?

Actually, yes, two more cautions. Don't bury it. Don't burn it. Burning was the accepted practice for some years, but the thinking on this has now changed. No matter how careful you think you may be, one accidental forest fire is one too many. Use as little paper, therefore, as you can manage and then pack it all out. To better encourage this practice when camped with others, it's helpful to provide instructions and a discreet location for collection. A paper bag can be stationed at the outer edge of camp along with a shovel and a roll of t.p.

It goes without saying that you should also pack out all other inorganic accouterments of toiletry: tampons, sanitary pads, and diapers. If you are washing diapers on a trip, dispose of the actual ca-ca in one-sit holes dug in the manner previously described. Haul the wash bucket above the high water line and use only biodegradable soap. In rinsing out the wash bucket, use another pan or bucket to avoid rinsing directly in a stream. Pour the wash water into a hole (again, above the high water line) and cover with dirt. Even with bio-degradable soap, don't wash directly in a watercourse.

The digging of a group latrine may be indicated on rare occasions. I cringe at the thought of sharing how to build latrines, and for that reason did not include it in the first edition of this book. More than several people have since inquired. With the idea that it is better for a person to have the best information and not use it, than to ignorantly spade up random plots, I have laid it all out here — though not without considerable trepidation. Large, concentrated deposits of fecal matter break down extremely slowly. You mustn't head into the woods with the casual thought, "Oh, we'll just dig a big old pit." Excavating a latrine will disturb a large area of plant life. In many places now-adays a latrine will be environmentally inappropriate; you will need to come prepared to pack out all the human waste your group generates (again see Chapter Three).

It is the highly unusual circumstance that requires a latrine. One situation comes to mind: I was recently reminded there is an age, somewhere between childhood and adulthood, characterized by squeamishness and fits of giggling embarrassment. Usually groups of this maturity remain close to trailhead or base camp facilities. If you find yourself in the boondocks the leader of such a group, and you're not sufficiently assured that cat holes will be dug in a proper manner, then a latrine may be in order. When you are giving out instructions, keep in mind that embarrassment and squeamishness are cultural phenomena that will not disappear until adults become more direct in their own approach to the subject.

Think of a latrine as a multi-person cat hole, as opposed to a coffin-sized trench. It needs to be easily accessible, closer to camp than a cat hole would be, and with some type of screening provided for privacy. The rest of the location considerations are similar to cat holes. Choose a spot a good distance from all watercourses and well above a river's high water line. Stay far away from boggy areas, springs, meadows, wetlands of any sort, and 200 feet from lakes. Keep out of dry washes that might carry storm runoff. In other words, again go for the high ground. Stop a minute, study the terrain, and visualize where water might flow. Even in a desert there are signs: slick rocks are a give-away, water had probably polished them.

Situate the latrine in soil with exceptionally good humus. The disadvantages of large deposits are a higher concentration of pathogens in one place and a slower rate of breakdown. Excavate a shallow (six- to eight-inch), narrow (nine- to ten-inch) trench that people can straddle and squat over. To determine the length of your latrine, you must take into account the size of your group and the length of stay. Underestimate — you can always dig up a few more feet. Pile the dirt alongside the length of the trench. Instruct people to begin at one end; after each deposit, shovel in a dusting, stir energetically, cover well, and tamp down. A communal stick for stirring can be conveniently left sticking into the used section of the trench, stirring end down. Ever hear of the expression "shit end of the stick?" This is the stick they were talking about (in the old days, it had a rag attached to one end for cleaning chamber pots). Finally, leave a paper bag for refuse handy to the squatter. Later it will be packed out or burned in the campfire.

In the end, we all have a decision to make about our sanitary methods. The procedure we choose will depend upon the size of our group, the maturity and agility of its members, the type of terrain, the season and climate, the remoteness of location, the visitor volume, and on and on. The easier we make it for ourselves, the harder it will be on Mother Earth. For those of us who grew up on the "P.U.s!" of western civilization's toiletries, it's going to require a fair portion of determination at some bends in the trail. But take heart, we're all learning together — about something we all do.

◆

Ocean saltwater is a different story than fresh water. It is customary when sea kayaking to void in a can, toss the contents overboard, rinse out the can, and resume paddling. Or, if it is warm enough, you can jump overboard, provided you are practiced in solo rescue and can get back in. On ecological grounds some sea touring groups recommend water disposal, even for *number two*, over waiting for a beach disposal.

On first thought, the idea of depositing one's excretia in water ran contrary to all environmental fibers in my being. Recollection of a water experience in Mexico reinforces my resistance. Someone once handed me a cheap ticket to Acapulco and I arrived on the lovely tropical beaches only to be warned not to go swimming in the bay's polluted waters — too much raw sewage, it seemed. When the heat became oppressive, I swam in the hotel's chlorinated pool — kind of like being at the Y at home. As you might understand, it is with undying reluctance that I put forth these poop and dump procedures for ocean kayakers. Nevertheless, I have been informed that the ocean is quite capable of breaking down a few turds.

A kayak, after all, is but a one-person/one-coffee-can yacht. If you consider the small number of sea kayakers bobbing around in a vast ocean, then dumping out your can in the water seems a fair practice. I promise, I won't worry about it. I'll worry about the Queen Mary-sized cruise ships flushing their holding tanks, about coastal towns worldwide running raw sewage into the sea, about oil spills, about barrels of toxic waste, about balloons turning up in dead marine animals' intestines, about the price of scallops . . . and such. That's enough to worry about.

I don't suppose anyone will be attempting the first of these water disposal maneuvers (using the can) within sight of a crowded beach, since the balance and verve of an Olympic pommel horse performer are required to shit in a can while afloat in a kayak, not to mention what's needed if you're wearing a wet suit. In any case, whether you use a can or jump overboard, it's only sensible to stay away from small bays, harbors, and any beaches where sludge might wash ashore before breaking up. By federal law, ocean-going vessels are prohibited from dumping sewage unless three miles offshore. There are boaters who argue that the disposal of shit in water around island communities is safe when tossed into a moving, deep-water column of twelve feet or more. Yet the casual vacation kayaker (me) paddling in a maze of channels may find it difficult to ascertain depth beneath a bobbing boat. What's more, a knowledge of tides is involved or, instead of flushing out to sea, your "turd overboard" could wash right back onto favored clam beds.

Sea kayakers are paddling our coasts in ever increasing numbers, typically touring close to islands and weaving through estuaries where wildlife viewing is best. It is this author's recommendation, on a planet already overburdened with excrement, that no fecal matter be tossed overboard inside the three mile zone of a mainland or the most seaward island in a group of islands. *Packing-it-out*, transporting it home for sewage treatment, is the preferred course of action. There is no law that says sea kayakers can't set the example for the Queen Marys of the world. There will come a time — if it hasn't come already — when the ocean, itself, says "Enough!"

Remember, both of the above techniques for ocean disposal require practice — dry runs, so to speak — on calm waters at home. Indeed, you have a valuable companion when someone will steady your boat for you while gallantly refusing to peek. If you're planning to paddle a two-seater — unless you're unruffable, or endowed with great panache — better hope that you draw the rear seat. As with any new camp practice — setting up a tent, for instance — test it out with your partner before setting out to sea like the Owl and the Pussycat in your beautiful pea-green boat.

WHEN YOU CAN'T DIG A HOLE

In days of old
When knights were bold
And toilets weren't invented,
They left their load
Along the road
And walked off so contented.

A childhood ditty; author unknown

In the pursuit of unknowns, a ranging world explorer can throw open entire new universes, not to mention some curious dimensions of toiletry and disposal. Sometimes there's just no place to dig a hole. Most of us never have occasion to pray that we won't have to go big potty outside when it's forty below or while dangling in midair between pitons on a hundred-foot rock face. In all probability, we are home knitting or walking the dog. Of course, anyone trudging on foot to the South Pole or climbing Mount Everest is already committed to a multitude of unpleasantries. These breeds of outdoor enthusiasts are extraordinary souls and pride in their accomplishments does not spring from enduring the ordinary. The morning constitutional behind the morning paper is an ordinary, even enjoyable, task when performed at home. But under adverse conditions, this simple activity can turn into a colossal calamity or feat of contortion. Consider the mishap Chris Bonington endured at 26,000 feet during an ascent on Everest, as described in his book *The Ultimate Challenge* (New York: Stein & Day, 1963):

> Now we've got these one-piece down suits; it's not too bad, in fact it's comparatively easy to relieve oneself when wearing the down suit by itself. If, however, you are wearing the down suit and the outer suit, it is absolutely desperate, trying to get the two slits to line up. . . . Afterwards, without thinking, without looking back, I stood up and shoved my windproof suit back on. . . . I did not realize anything was wrong — until I poked my hand through the cuff! I tried to scrape it off — rub it off — but by this time the sun had gone, it was bitterly cold and it had frozen to the consistency of concrete.

And take note of this poor woman, who also bought a suit of misery. A demented (my substitute for the explorer's adjective *robust*) friend of mine was camped on Oregon's Three Sisters during a blizzard when an imperious peristaltic contraction indicated it was time to crawl out of the tent and squat. So — out she crawled into a complete whiteout, with snow blowing horizontally on a wicked wind. Five layers of clothes had to be stripped from her rosy behind and shoved below her knees. Never mind the freezing, in retrieving her pants she found that each layer, not unlike a bird bath, had captured a supply of snow. Once the clothes were again clasped to her body, the snow began to melt. Winter campers call it the "soggies." When questioned as to whether she might not have some helpful hint for others caught in such circumstances, her only reply came, "Hold it!"

Yet two timeworn solutions to the undeniable problems associated with winter camping do offer themselves. Trap doors decidedly provide some buttress against inclement weather. Fashioned after the old union suits with their buttoned fanny drop-flaps, various styles are now available in heavy expedition wear. We thank Bonnington for sharing his predicament; it provides solace after the fact for those in the misery-loves-company category and serves to forewarn the rest of us of one disastrous route to humiliation.

The other merciful aid in sub-zero temperatures? Just what *did* great grandma do when it was too bitter to pad along in her bare feet and flannel nightie to the outhouse? Of course: the old porcelain chamber pot — the thunder mug as it was called. Less elegantly, coffee cans have been used. A friend of mine who's an expedition leader was caught once in rush hour gridlock on the fourth level of a freeway interchange. Fortunately it was only a *number one* emergency; he filled his thermos four times and casually dumped the contents out the window. Also, I hear from a reliable female source that Tupperware bread savers have been put to the same good use on long cross-country hauls across barren landscapes.

◆

As I sit here tapping out this chapter on a state-of-the-art computer, hundreds of barrels of frozen turds and urine lie around McMurdo Station, Antarctica — looking for a home. The general garbage situation in McMurdo, our major U.S. South Pole science station, is an "unseemly story," a mountain "hideous to behold," as the *San Francisco Examiner* reports. By the time you read this chapter — who knows — some of these barrels may very well be thawing in your own home town.

If our wilderness world is to survive the onslaught of use (misuse) and overuse in the coming years, we must find better means for disposing of human waste. The numbers of both hardy explorers and more casual backcountry travelers continues to swell around the globe — and so does the volume of excrement. In many respects, we are still grappling with the identical sanitation problems of T. J. Crapper's nineteenth century. Too much stuff, no good place for it to go. No matter how conscientious people become about packing out food garbage and trash to the major trail heads (and in some places they are), still each wave, in addition to footprints, leaves deposits of poop. You can only cram so many apples in a barrel and then the barrel is full.

The burgeoning feeling in the outdoor community is we can no longer afford — like knights of old — to leave our load along the road. One example, grievously noticeable to early spring backpackers, is the human waste of the previous season's visitors. After the snow melts, frozen lumpettes left by cross-country skiers sit plunk on top of the ground. As the weather warms, they thaw and ripen along with the rest of the landscape. For the early hiker seeking a few days solace in untrammeled places, this is a horrific sight. One might better have stayed home and scheduled a tour at the local sewage treatment plant.

There's no question that improperly cared for waste can be a fierce affront to our aesthetics and a threat to our health. But at other times, leaving behind even the most properly buried deposits can cause irreparable ecological damage. Small islands have tenuous ecosystems at best. Fragility is inherent: islands have no adjacent support system. Off the coast of Maine lie three thousand islands, many no bigger than an acre. The interdependence of life on an acre-island — what looks to us to be grasses and a couple of trees — has been in the making for millions of years. Now visitors come and not just in the form of the odd fisherman or lovers picnicking, but sea kayakers by the dozen camping overnight and tour groups off chartered schooners, sometimes thirty at a time, stopping for a landside lunch. Too many cat holes, too much disturbed earth, and the grasses vanish, leaving topsoil to the mercy of wind and weather. It is better for us to tread gently than to be confronted later with another in the long line of mitigations — not always successful mitigations — we now face.

The ecosystems of caves are another example of isolated and delicately balanced flora and fauna. Caves shelter vulnerable and delightfully bizarre little creatures found nowhere else on earth. For the spelunker, in addition to concern about survival of species-interdependence, there is the compelling subject of rank odors. The true cave-lover looks on the removal of bodily waste as merely one step in heedful exploration.

Packing-it-out — the practice of capturing and carrying fecal waste and sometimes pee out of the backcountry — is increasingly becoming a practical alternative to burial. Cal Adventures, the outdoor program at the University of California at Berkeley, under the direction of Rick Spittler in 1988, began experimenting with containerization systems for individual skiers in their cross-country skiing program. Their novel techniques were successful, if rudimentary: milk cartons with duct tape. Today, on both the east and west coasts of North America, concerned sea kayakers are inventing ways to cart their human waste home. The U.S. Forest Service is strapping portable toilets onto mules that accompany trail crews into the mountains. The big outdoor schools, Colorado Outward Bound (COB) and the National Outdoor Leadership School (NOLS), are teaching packing-it-out in sensitive environments and high use areas. Even rock-climbers (fed up with oversized hail?) are changing their ways. We'll return later to the plight of the individual poop packer — our focus for the rest of this chapter will be groups and their portable shitarees.

Parties of wilderness travelers have been addressing the problem of hauling human waste out of pristine areas for years, and whitewater boaters have long been at the forefront. River terrain poses a unique problem, with camping naturally confined along the limited beaches of steep and narrow canyons. Some twenty-five years ago, when whitewater boating began to grow in popularity, the increase in human visitation was subsequently followed by tremendous concentrations of fecal matter. The need to pack-it-out became evident when a person began turning over someone else's "stuff" in an effort to bury their own.

The River Permit Office for the Grand Canyon issues two full pages of instructions to trip leaders about packing out human waste. There is a potential for 200,000 deposits per year on Canyon beaches, roughly 50,000 tons of shit. Imagine, purely for the sake of comprehension, finding 200,000 helpings of spaghetti and meatballs buried in the sand — and with that picture the National Park Service's regulations become perfectly understandable. Since 1979 all solid human waste from Grand Canyon river trips has been containerized and packed out in water-tight boxes. No trip is allowed on the river without acceptable and ample holding tanks, proper education, and a commitment to pack-it-out.

The same is true now on other heavily used rivers. Packing-it-out was adopted in 1983 on Idaho's Main Salmon (Lewis and Clark's famed River of No Return), and at that time Bob Abbott, now district ranger of Nez Perce National Forest, was nothing short of skeptical about public cooperation. As a second generation ranger, born even in a ranger district, Abbott had already spent a lifetime observing *Homo sapiens* behavior in the wild. The Tin Can Tourist, as litterbugs were called in the days before plastic, couldn't be counted on to pack out even the smallest bits of trash. Abbott's reaction to the idea of expecting visitors to haul out their excrement was "You gotta be kidding! We'll have shit from hell to breakfast!" Today he's a convert and emanates downright pride when he says, "You can visit a beach that's had three thousand visitors in the space of a few months and see no sign that humans have been there."

As more backcountry spots become overrun with visitation comparable to river canyons, more packing-it-out will be required. And as if to assure this, there's clear evidence that county, state, and federal governments are all tightening sewage disposal regulations. For example, in Washington State's King County, a one hundred-page Sensitive Areas Ordinance creates buffer zones of twenty-five to one hundred feet around three different classifications of wetlands, ruling out among other things, septic systems. The ordinance contains no specifications for an individual camper's deposits, nonetheless, local environmentally minded sea kayakers using cat hole methods, find occasion for the joke, "Know your wetland plants!" Not so easy, according to King County environmental educator Ken Carrasco. "Of all the environmentally sensitive areas, the most difficult to delineate and classify are wetlands." Wetland plants are not only the obvious swampy specimens of eelgrass and cattails; western red cedar, black cottonwood, and Sitka spruce are often found in "forested wetlands." Only seven days of inundation during the growing season (March to November in the Seattle area) are necessary to set the stage for survival of a wetland species. Wetlands can vary greatly in size, some taking up no more than the space needed for an office file cabinet. To quote a chapter heading from the Army Corps of Engineers' publication *Wetland Plants of the Pacific Northwest*: "Wetland Identification Complexities: Life is Not Simple."

Examples of tightening regulations at the state level can be found in Washington's Department of Ecology (DOE). Philip KauzLoric, dairy waste coordinator for the Water Quality Program, says, "Water quality agencies across the country that for twenty years have emphasized the upgrading of sewage treatment plants now are turning their focus to 'nonpoint' sources of pollution involving overland run-off." Larger scale dairy and cattle-raising operations are increasingly required to meet existing state and federal water pollution control standards that affect public surface waters — waters the public uses for swimming, fishing, shellfish fishing, and community water supplies. It's a program, so to speak, of keeping those cow pie Frisbees out of the crick! There is a new field staff at the DOE assigned specifically to complaints of agricultural pollution. Theirs is a touchy job, insisting that farmers who historically retain water rights must now develop management plans for watering livestock without destroying water quality. Pasture rotation and fencing (a new version of a traditionally hot issue in the West) are often what's called for.

At the federal level is a recently formed task force, Human Waste Management of Federal Lands, comprised of six government agencies and headed by LuVerne Grussing of the Idaho Bureau of Land Management. The task force has set up a pilot project that is in part a response to a new ruling by another federal agency. In October 1993, the Environmental Protection Agency (EPA) outlawed the dumping of human fecal matter into landfills, and though not a law enacted with wilderness goers in mind, it greatly affects us. An EPA representative I spoke with said, "Sewage must go where it can be treated — into sewage treatment plants, sewers, or septic tanks."

For some years the classic toilet system for river runners had been an inexpensive ($15) WWII ammunition can, commonly called an *ammo can* or *rocket box*. The can's lid clamped down vice-like onto a rubber gasket creating a secure seal against spillage. When in use, the can was lined with a plastic garbage bag and a toilet seat positioned on top — it was presto, outdoor potty! (On gear-light private trips, the toilet seat was often omitted, which led to the nickname *groover* from the indentations left in a sitter's bum.)

With recycled rocket boxes, boaters hauled virtually millions of tons of human waste out of the wilderness. But always awaiting them at the take-out were a few glitches. Invariably at a trip's end, there were no facilities equipped to receive bagged shit. (Plastic bags don't biodegrade rapidly and are incompatible with septic tanks and sewage treatment plants. They particularly gum up the works in the honey wagons that pump out trailhead outhouses.)

After caring for their cargoes of turds — painstakingly removing them from camps, ferrying them down rivers, bearing them across beaches, and packing them into vehicles — stymied rafters hurled a goodly percentage of those bulging bags into open pits on south forties. At best, the bags were trucked for miles to a sewage treatment plant where the contents were poured out, the soiled bags bagged again and dropped into the trash. At worst, and not uncommon, were the woeful tales from river guides who thought they were doomed to driving a vehicle permanently laden with the infamous bags. Many a moonless landscape, a handy dumpster, or a lonesome spot in the road caught their share of "fling it and runs." There is something terribly awry when the most environmentally conscious bunch around — whitewater boaters — are stuck with no better solution.

The EPA, as some see it, has come to the rescue. Its recent ruling confronted, however inadvertently, the big void (pun intended) in sewage facilities at take-outs and trailheads. The regulation forces us to progress beyond plastic garbage bags, as even if you were to pour the fecal matter down the pipe at an R.V. station, you must still contend with the soiled bag. Prohibited from sending it to a landfill, what *do* you do? Not everyone has the iron stomach required to launder one.

As might be guessed with new frontiers and creativity the adventurer's eternal callings, rising to the occasion is a spate of inventors, all scurrying to produce a washable, re-usable container that's also user-friendly — as in requiring the least holding of the nose. Jeff Kellogg of Clavey Equipment tells me a new design appears almost every week. Before we examine these new-fangled portable holding tanks, another invention deserves our attention.

It's the giant **SCAT Machine** (from Frenchglen Blacksmiths, Highway 205, Frenchglen, OR 97736, phone 503-495-2315), essentially an industrial-sized dishwasher hooked into a sewer system. Inventors John and Cindy Witzel say their design will accept almost any of the portable holding tanks: a container must have at least an eight-inch top opening and a recommended minimum height of 13" (containers with a height of 11 3/4" to 12" work marginally, but anything shorter will not dump properly). The SCAT Machine neatly dumps handleless five gallon buckets or box-type containers when strapped down by the handles. The lids of the holding tanks are removed and also set inside the machine. Closing the machine causes it to swing through a one-eighty turn and dumps the holding tank's contents down the sewer. Drop a few quarters or tokens into a slot and the apparatus washes and sanitizes your tank and all but reaches out and hands it back to you. Installation sites require an existing sewer, septic, or leach line system, a 220 power source, and a water supply capable of forty-five gallons per use. SCAT Machines cost $15,800, delivered and installed within three hundred miles of the manufacturer. To date, three SCAT Machines have been acquired by federal agencies (the Bureau of Land Management, U.S. Forest Service, and National Park Service) and serve mostly river runners in their respective locations of Meadview, Arizona; Asotin, Washington; and Riggins, Idaho. Two more machines are in the works for Diamond Creek, Arizona and Salmon, Idaho.

There *is* one alternative — in case you're wondering — to all this lugging around of poop. Though not something I personally recommend, I present it here and leave it for you to decide. The suggestion arrived in one of the many letters I receive — a correspondent I've since duly dubbed the Enema Man. In a short typed note, he graciously shares his practice of holing up in a motel to flush his colon the night before striking out for a weekend of fishing. This enables him to roam about untroubled by the particulars of how to squat in the woods, leaving him to concentrate solely on his sport, while — he writes in all sincerity — simultaneously "avoid[ing] polluting the streams and their environs." If this appeals to you, read no further. Hand this book to a neighbor! The rest of us, even with the knowledge that here very well may lie the solution to a world of problems, will, nonetheless, move on to examining holding tanks.

I am listing the manufacturers of wilderness toilets because most are small operations and sell by mail order. Though I've added a few comments about each model, this is not meant to be an exhaustive evaluation; design revisions occur frequently and, to be fair, I haven't sat on all of them. The very act of plopping down on one reveals a critical characteristic — how readily the toilet tips over. And this, believe me, is important. Once a contraption containing the waste of fourteen people throws you to the ground and tries to drown you, there's a good chance you'll turn into a couch potato for life.

When purchasing a portable toilet, there are numerous things to watch for and weigh. Pick and choose between design features that most suit you. You can't have everything with the cheaper products. In general, you get more with the higher priced systems but so far, it seems, nothing's perfect.

Off the top there are four important things to consider: your health, container stability, "disgust factor," and price. Starting with the last and simplest, present prices range from $15 to $540. I've presented them in order from high end to low. The few companies that rent toilets are noted. One requirement for Grand Canyon river trips is that your human waste carry-out assembly be "of value" dollar-wise, for the simple reason that less full containers are then casually discarded, tucked behind a cactus somewhere. The River Permit Office has their own list of approved manufacturers, which is ever changing as new products come on the market. For a copy, write to U.S. Department of Interior, National Park Service, Grand Canyon National Park, P.O. Box 129, Grand Canyon, Arizona 86023-0129.

The river guides I know wear latex gloves when drawing the short straw for potty duty — a wise precaution, but also one lamentably ironic. Proud as we are about diminishing our consumption of plastic bags, we seem to be tying our next Gordian knot around a mountain of latex gloves. But health is definitely the priority for the clean-out staff. The handling of human waste is not a business to be taken lightly, and any potential for direct exposure to fecal matter during the emptying and cleaning processes should be carefully considered.

Some holding tanks, upon opening, will "burp in your face." Methane gas is a natural by-product of anaerobic decomposing feces. Be forewarned: a sealed holding tank — full or partially full — left in the sun can blow up. Fireworks of that caliber have the potential to psychologically brand a person for life. Short of explosion, tanks can also bubble and cough and emit world-class farts. Having an automatic pressure-release mechanism is a decided advantage on long or hot-weather trips. If yours is a courageous spirit, however, tanks without pressure-release valves generally are cheaper and you can crack the lid occasionally, remembering to pack your gear so the lid is accessible. Be advised that peeing in the potty contributes to methane build-up, but not peeing in it may make the dumping difficult at trip's end. There are two schools of thought on content consistency: the wet and the dry. The wet group believes in brewing a sort of slurry that, when the time comes, will pour easily. Thus sometimes, the women of a trip are instructed to pee in the pot; other times, guests are told to pee elsewhere, and the guides discreetly monitor and maintain a proper consistency. The dry group, acutely aware that liquids add to weight, prefers to collect only solid waste, adding water at the completion of a trip, or sometimes never, as in the case when the container is made of pressed paper.

Next to ponder is shape: round, square, oblong. Consider your load (that is, how your gear is packed). A round object, if not entirely sturdy, may eventually assume a square shape when squished by a heavy load. Also buckets with bottoms smaller in diameter than their tops are going to be less stable to sit on than a container of squatter and squarer design.

Other high priorities are sturdiness in construction material and top-of-the-line seals at all the openings. If a boat flips in a "mother" rapid, there should be no chance of a holding tank breaking open upon impact with an untimely boulder or its seals leaking during "maytagging" at the bottom of a sous hole. Seals must pass what I'm now calling the Donny Dove Test. DDT has a whole new meaning. Dove is Canyon REO's (River Equipment Outfitters) expert on leakage. A man with a purpose, he packs a gallon of water seemingly wherever he goes, pouring it into the latest inventions and turning them upside-down. Dove espouses a simple but profound axiom: If it can't hold water, it shouldn't hold shit! At last count, not all passed his test. One more thing to be said about material is that plastics may retain odors. Stainless steel and aluminum are generally more easily cleaned and there is no chance of their drying and cracking with extended exposure to the sun.

Eventually, you must think about the end of your trip and the task of dumping the holding tank. Compatibility with the SCAT Machine is a plus when you are planning to be near one of the few on the planet, but compatibility with R.V. dumping stations is a *must*. The latter is achieved by attaching a garden hose at one opening, a sewer hose at another, and blasting fresh water through the tank. Some tanks are not equipped with orifices that fit the fresh water hose exactly. Instead, the flushing is accomplished through the larger toilet seat hole, which can produce unsanitary splash back. This can be remedied somewhat by fashioning a large rubber washer through which you insert the hose.

Sewage cleaning services come highly recommended as a way of entirely avoiding the cleanout chore. With this news, I called around the rural area where I live and found no such service. I was, in fact, alarmed to discover that the portable plastic outhouses, the ones seen lined up at all manner of public events, were cleaned merely with squirts of cold water. Towns near take-outs for popular river runs are probably better bets. In any case, it's worth the call — if nothing else, it may inspire someone to propose an updating of public health standards. Another choice for disposal is a sewage treatment plant. There the contents of the holding tank are poured through an open grate but the mucking out of the container is left to you.

If your group is large or your trip is long, you will need more than one holding tank. When calculating volume, you *must* allow not only for actual space but for what is termed "disgust factor." Using the same container for more than two or three days, or until topped off, will nauseate almost anyone: in traditional approach/avoidance conflict, most of us instinctively peer down the hole before sitting. In addition, there are always the critical matters of tidal waves, splashes, and for gentlemen, the safety of those forever dangling darlings. Prized is the toilet seat mounting that provides for perching well above a can's contents. Deodorizers, or sweeteners as they're called, can also help minimize disgust factor.

The prices I've quoted are all retail; some include shipping. Any dimensions given are for holding tanks alone — sometimes inside measurements, sometimes outside — without a seat assembly on top. A "user-day" means one person, one day. In other words, fifty user-days can mean five people shitting for ten days or ten people shitting for five days, or even fifty people shitting for one day. Capacities noted are not calculated by any standardized method, but given in accordance with the manufacturer's advertising. Some are for poops per can, some for people per day no matter what they are eating, and some for full-to-the-brim tanks.

Try as I might, I found it difficult to establish what is an "average" poop. It's not the open and shut case implied by Woody Guthrie's infamous line in the movie *Bound for Glory*,

". . . the more you eat, the more you shit." In medical encyclopedias there is a hesitancy to commit to a one-figure average, the world-wide range of normalcy being broad. Anyone who takes a dump three to twenty-one times per week can be considered normal. The individual product is dependent on a person's age, size of physical frame, diet, gender, race, continent of residence, even personality. People who eat more fiber produce more bulk. Men, as a rule, produce more than women. A typical stool in India weighs three times that of one in England or in the United States, whereas in Uganda (where surely they eat bricks) turd poundage is five times greater. Those of us who survived the 1960s, pledged to the eternal process of "getting our shit together," may be disheartened to learn that though our shit may stink less now, it probably weighs more. The fifth edition of *Gastrointestinal Disease: Pathophysiology, Diagnosis, Management* by Sleisenger and Fordtran (Philadelphia: W. B. Saunders, 1993), tells us that people with high self-esteem produce heavier stools. There is a proverb or fortune cookie riddle in here somewhere, I know it. Something like: too much psychotherapy makes for weighty business! Thankfully, Carol Hupping Stoner takes a stab at averages for us in *Goodbye to the Flush Toilet: Water-Saving Alternatives to Cesspools, Septic Tanks, and Sewers* (Emmaus, PA: Rodale Press, 1977), calculating daaily human excrement at one half pound moist weight. That should help — the half pounder being an American institution.

A little more advice? Carry a gallon of water and ask lots of questions.

Washable, Re-usable Human Waste Carry-out Systems

The **Baño**, ($540 from Holiday River Expeditions, 544 East 3900 South, Salt Lake City, UT 84107, phone 801-266-2087). With a name befitting its southwest origins, The Baño is a molded plastic holding tank (same material as giant-sized garbage cans) with aluminum handles, stainless steel fasteners, and a hard plastic seat assembly. There are no rubber seals to clean; the lid and box mesh together in a tapered manner with a lock-down clamp. Also included in the price is the cleanout apparatus for R.V. dumping stations (clamp-on funnel with sewer hose, garden hose fitting, and built-in power spray nozzle). The tank is a stable design (14" x 17" x 12½" height), slightly smaller than two 30mm rocket boxes. It weighs 15.1 pounds when totally assembled, and has a capacity of fifty user-days. The outfit lacks a pressure release valve, but I'm told there is some flex to the box. Additional tanks cost $300, and a herculite storage bag for the toilet seat is $24. The Green River, Utah, outlet of Holiday River Expeditions rents The Baño for $25 (one to three days), $45 (four to seven days), $2 per day thereafter, and $5 for the seat assembly. Compatibility with the SCAT Machine has not been established (it's questionable with any tank under 13" in height). The Baño is used by Colorado Outward Bound.

The *Jon-ny Partner* ($445 from Partner Steel Company, 3187 Pole Line Road, Pocatello, ID 83201, phone 208-233-2371). Here we have what many call the Cadillac of portable toilets, a bomb-proof stainless steel holding tank. The price includes the tank with automatic pressure release value and three-inch opening for fresh water flushing, transport lid with rubber gasket and collar-clamp, toilet seat with lid, and flush kit (a clamp-on funnel with sewer hose) for R.V. dumping stations. It's also easily compatible with the SCAT Machine. Additional tanks cost $259. Stout handles at seat level on either side, coupled with a square design (12" x 12" x 17" height), assure stability in seating even for the most graceless among us. Capacity is fifty to sixty user-days, calculated at twenty-seven cubic inches per person per day, based on a study of boaters who ate such things as pork chops and omelets for breakfast. Dry weight is twenty pounds, ninety when full. The toilet seat has a flange that fits down inside the box and provides additional stability when in use, but may require cleaning before packing away. The Jon-ny Partner is used by commercial and private boaters on many western rivers, by the Forest Service trail crews in Idaho, and by hunting parties in base camps. Customizing is welcomed; ask for Harvey Partner, the man himself.

The *Green Machine* ($285 from HEADGEAR, 1428 Warner Avenue, Lewiston, ID 83501, phone 208-743-0625). An "industrial quality" seat/tank unit, this one is made of chemical resistant, laminated fiberglass resin with marine-grade fasteners and handles. The base is the size of two 20mm ammo cans (18" x 20" x 14½" height). The tank has a one-half inch garden hose fitting, which serves as the venting system when in camp, and a three-inch sewer cleanout with accompanying sewer hose. Dry weight is seventeen pounds, one hundred when full, with a capacity of 12.5–14 gallons or 125– 200 user-days (based on solid waste deposits only). It's a stable unit and SCAT Machine compatible. The seat lid also functions as the lock-down transport lid and may require cleaning after a day of running heavy whitewater. Designer Curtis Chang welcomes customizing and will adapt tank sizes for specific packing requirements. Green Machines have been used since 1983 by Northwest Dories, Chang's river touring company, and by the Curry Company in Yosemite National Park.

The **Human Waste Tank** ($265 from Waterman Welding, 2552 US 89A South, Kanab, UT 84741, phone 801-644-5729). The standard size (14" x 21" x 12" height) for this marine-grade, corrosion resistant, aluminum container fits in the space of two 20mm ammo cans. But for custom building any size to suit you, ask for Scott Dunn. A river guide in the Grand Canyon before packing-it-out become regulation, Dunn was one of the first to promote containerization. He remembers the park service landing at his camp more than twenty years ago on one of their routine inspections just when he was experimenting with an ammo can and a plastic bag. "They gave me not so good grades on canyon descriptions," he says, "but rated me right at the top on human waste." The Human WasteTank was originally designed in 1972 by Ron Smith of Grand Canyon Expeditions who was ahead of his time with a washable, reusable container. The tank has an automatic pressure release valve and three-inch cleanout drain, a transport cap with lock-ring, a seat mount, and top handles that don't interfere with adjacent gear. A ten-inch diameter top hole with a three-inch high collar makes it SCAT Machine compatible. To empty at R.V. dumping stations you need the flush apparatus ($69), which is an inverted funnel with garden hose fitting that secures to the tank with the transport cap's lock-ring. You must buy your own sewer hose, clamp, and toilet seat. Poop capacity is fifteen gallons, well over one hundred user-days. Spare tanks are $205.50. This is a system for large parties, but a determined non-commercial group of ten, I was told, could get by on one tank for as long as ten days. The unit is lightweight for its size (twelve pounds), but good muscle should be available to move it when full. Sold to both commerial and private parties.

I particularly like the name of the next one. It's the **MAGIC GROOOVER**, after the seatless ammo can that left furrows in your bum ($255 from Magic Groover, P.O. Box 638, Westminster, CO 80030, phone 303-657-1779). David Waddle has designed a stainless steel box around the idea that throwing away all the old 20mm rocket boxes is wasteful, thus his container fits perfectly inside one. It is also functional on its own, but then requires fashioning a means for tying it down and for a carrying handle. The tank has a three-inch bayonet cleanout drain (a quarter turn releases it), a three-fourth inch fresh water hose fitting, and an automatic pressure release valve. Included are the sewer hose and a standard toilet seat with a lid. The system is compatible with the SCAT Machine and R.V. dumping stations; in the latter circumstance, a built-in power spray nozzle blasts the inside while the quick-release top lid remains sealed, virtually assuring the handler of zero exposure to fecal matter. Capacity is fifty user-days; dry weight is ten pounds, fifty when full. Spare tanks run $185. The MAGIC GROOOVER fits nicely into a packhorse panyard and is used by the Colorado and Utah Bureau of Land Management on river patrols and fish studies, by climbers at desert base camps, and by junior high school classes at field biology camps. David's sister who works for the U.S. Postal Service is plotting to put one in her mail truck.

The **River Bank** ($215 from Septic Bank, 1213 Thousand Springs Grade, Wendell, ID 83355, phone 208-536-5368) is an obvious play on words as well as a subtly apt name as unlike cat holes, which must be located well above the high water line, a portable john can sit right at river's edge. The molded box/toilet seat affair (16" x 16" x 17" height) has a nesting five gallon bucket as the holding tank. There's room in the box to store toilet paper, deodorizers, and cleaning supplies (which with any system must be stored somewhere). Included with the box/seat unit and seat lid are an eight-foot sewer hose and the bucket with a sewer spout three-inches in diameter. In the spout's cap is a pressure release valve. New for 1994 is the bucket's clamp-on-type transport lid equipped with a fresh water hose fitting for flushing. With the exception of the sewer hose, the items are made of soft polyethylene, "kayak plastic." Additional bucket seats cost $75. The bucket's dry weight is seven pounds, thirty to forty pounds when full, with capacity calculated at thirty user-days (filled to a level of three gallons). Both box and bucket have convenient handle/tie-downs. A five gallon bucket with plain screw-type lid ($15) is also available, and both buckets are SCAT Machine compatible. The River Bank is used by Hughes River Expeditions and on mountain pack trips out of an Idaho dude ranch.

The **D-Can,** alias BP-Can for bomb-proof ($148 from Canyon REO, P.O. Box 3493, Flagstaff, AZ 86003, phone 800-637-4604), are retrofitted ammo cans. New 25mm surplus cans (17½" x 10" x 14½" height) are two and one-half inches wider and more stable than the 20mm. The cans are coated inside with an easily cleaned polyurethane "rhino lining" and fitted with a welded top/seat opening. A double safety seal on the transport lid is "Donny Dove" guaranteed not to leak. The can is SCAT Machine compatible, and for an additional $10, you can have a receptacle installed that accepts a sewer hose for cleaning at R.V. dump stations. The fresh water flush is accomplished through the ten-inch diameter seat opening. Dry weight is twenty-six pounds, with a capacity of seventy to eighty user-days ("hero use" up to 100). The can is not equipped with a pressure release valve and you buy your own sewer hose and toilet seat. You can also rent D-Cans, with or without a toilet seat, for $1.50 per day. The best is that for $12.50, at the end of your trip, you are allowed to return a rental can chockfull to Canyon REO, turn your back, and walk away. If you want to be bothered, for slightly less per can, there are Flagstaff sewer services that will dump, steam clean, and disinfect tanks (see listings after PRO Ammo Cans). D-Cans are used by Arizona Raft Adventures and sold to private boaters all over the country.

Coyote Bagless Toilet Systems ($120 from Four Corners River Sports, P.O. Box 379, Durango, CO 81302, phone 800-426-7637). The polyethylene box (12" x 12" x 14" height) has a separate raised toilet seat assembly. The design change for 1994 is a screw-top transport lid with gasket. Dry weight is nine pounds with a capacity for fifty-five user-days. The system includes the holding tank with a three-inch drain hole, a transport/cleanout lid with a ¾-inch garden hose fitting, a plastic toilet seat (without lid), and a ten-inch sewer hose, fitting, and hose clamp. Spare tanks with three-inch cleanout drains and simple transport lids are $65. The outfit is compatible with R.V. dump stations and the SCAT Machine, but is minus a pressure release valve. The transport lid serves as the seat cover while in camp, and in place of handles, a lip around the top provides the means for carrying. Tie-downs were in the thinking stage when I spoke with their representative. On the plus-side, the Coyote Bagless Toilet System has a lightweight stable design and the price is right. Sells mostly to non-commercial boaters.

The **Scat Packer** ($89.95 from Wilson Enterprises, 18660 South Greenview Drive, Oregon City, OR 97045, phone 503-631-3844). "It's a FACT, PACK your SCAT!" is the advertisement. This one is a lightweight, high density polyethylene bucket (14" x 14" diameter). It weighs three and a half pounds, forty-five pounds when full with a capacity of forty user days. It has a screw-type transport lid with a safety lock. Included is a customized seat mount, a full-sized toilet seat with a lid, and a sanitary waste transfer lid equipped with a garden hose fitting, cleanout drain, and sewer hose. Additional buckets cost $26.25. Storing in the shade or occasionally cracking the lid is recommended, as the unit is not equipped with a pressure release valve. There is also the **Scat Packer Junior** ($74.95, 12" x 11½" diameter) for day use. The Junior has one half the capacity but the same accessories except for the seat mount. Additional containers cost $20.70. A tiedown harness of one-inch nylon webbing ($10) is available for either size Scat Packer. Both units can be emptied at R.V. dumping stations; the full-sized bucket is SCAT Machine compatible. This is a system suitable for small groups, or refreshingly, changed daily with larger parties. Sold to boaters all over the country.

The **Porta Potti** is manufactured by the Thetford Corporation. This is the company that coined the word we now toss around so universally. The Porta Potti is an integral seat/tank assembly with a handle and a pour spout. Though dandy for R.V.s, trailers, and boats, it was not designed for river rafting or backcountry travel. A water/chemical flush system adds to weight while diminishing capacity in the holding tank. Without an additional securely sealing transport container, leakage may be a problem. Several sizes are available in discount stores. I located the smallest version (5¼" x 14" x 15" height), Model 155, on sale for $69.96. It weighs nine and a half pounds and holds 2.6 gallons of fresh water with a holding tank capacity of 4.3 gallons that boasts forty-five flushes.

Professional River Outfitters (PRO) Ammo Cans (1802 West Kaibab Lane, Flagstaff, AZ 86011, phone 602-779-1512) rents the traditional WWII 20mm ammo cans. For $1.50 per day (picked up in Flagstaff) you receive the ammo can, a toilet seat mounted on a flange that covers the top of the can, and a seat riser. Capacity is fifty to sixty deposits. Additional ammo cans rent for $0.50 per day and can be used for storage of non-food items such as charcoal and toilet paper before being employed as a holding tank. For those who already own 20mm ammo cans, PRO will sell you the toilet seat assembly ($60) and the seat riser ($60). At almost any surplus store, you can purchase an ammo can for $10 to $15 and be the proud owner of a piece of American history — in fact, several histories. Inspect the gasket to make certain it's in good shape and will be watertight: don't guess, test it. Bruce Helin, president of PRO Inc., recommends marking the cans and lids so "they can be kept together in the same orientation for best sealing." Ammo cans are SCAT Machine compatible; they can be dumped at sewage treatment plants, or you can buy a funnel that will allow you to pour the contents down the pipe at an R.V. station. In the latter two cases you are stuck with manually cleaning the can. For those who rent from PRO, the dumping and sterilizing chore can be taken off your hands, literally, for as little as $8.50 per can. For people with their own cans (or most any type of holding tank), two sewage services in Flagstaff will perform the same chores.

Contact **A-AARON'S Sanitation Service & Scotty's Potties** ($11 per can), 1860 West Kaibab Lane, Flagstaff, AZ 86001, phone 602-779-1767, or **Sandoval's Tanks a Lot** ($10 per can), 3200 North Fourth Street, Flagstaff, AZ 86004-2013, phone 602-526-0139. At Sandoval's, ask for Andy or Ralph. Their motto is "A flush beats a full house!"

Molded Fiber Toilet Liners, also known as Fiber Pots or Pickle Pail Liners ($5 or less from Western Pulp Wood Company, P.O. Box 968, Corvallis, OR 97339, phone 503-757-

1151). This unique biodegradable pot and lid is made out of recycled paper and comes with five additional form-fitting disks that are pressed into place over each day's deposits. A pot with accompanying dividers and a lid weighs one and a half pounds, twenty when full. To use they are placed inside five gallon pickle pails (condiment containers that restaurants typically discard), and a toilet seat is set on top. Capacity is twenty to twenty-five user-days (solid human waste, no pee). The Bureau of Land Management in Baker City, Oregon has been conducting a study on the wilderness use of fiber pots, handing them out to river runners on the Grand Ronde, Lower Salmon, and Snake Rivers. To facilitate disposal at the take-out, the BLM, with the help of Scheler Manufacturing, fabricated an electric grinder to attach to a holding tank on wheels ($10,000 altogether) that accepts the full pots. A manual grinder for backcountry locations, which would give the machine more versatility, was found to require a good twenty minutes of cranking per pot, but the BLM looks hopefully to the future and a solar generated crank. A distinct advantage with this system is that remote disposal locations require no sewer system, only a grinder/tank-on-wheels, or a grinder and in-ground holding tank similar to those of vault toilets, pumped out by a visiting honey wagon. Blessedly, with the Molded Fiber Toilet Liners, an outdoorperson's sole chore before heading down the road is to toss their intact package into the grinder.

Ammo can conversions and epoxy powder coatings and Guard Coat (from X-Stream Whitewater Boats, 4605 McLeod NE, Albuquerque, NM 87109, phone 505-881-2458). Ask for Stuart Rogers who believes in economy measures. For $12.50 you can buy a sewer fitting (bayonet drain) and install it yourself in an ammo can's lid to allow dumping at an R.V. station. Or for $25 (including the lid) X-Stream will install it for you. The converted lid is used only during dumping, as when packed on a boat or a mule the fitting can get in the way of other gear. For easy cleaning, X-Stream will bake an epoxy powder coating ($35–40) to the inside of an ammo can. Rogers cautions that this finish is only for the private boater who will clean the box carefully, because any scratches will soon rust. And dropping the can hard on a corner can shatter the finish. By talking to him further, you'll find he thinks the only good reason to powder coat is to meet the criteria of the river permit offices, some of which require boaters to have "sufficient financial commitment" to their holding tanks. For less money, X-Stream sells Guard Coat Series 200, a commercial coating used by the Coast Guard and Navy for corrosion proofing metal. It lasts up to thirty years in salt water environments and is a one-part product you can brush on. One-quart, $24.95, is enough to coat two ammo cans. Guard Coat contains acid modifiers that create a mechanical and chemical bond to metal. It takes more abuse than an epoxy powder surface, and scratches are easily repaired. To prepare the cans for coating, Rogers recommends rust remover jelly, then sanding or sand blasting. Or take the box to a radiator shop and have it dipped. An idea even less dear: use a pre-trip coating of common vegetable oil for easier cleaning later. Another Rogers' tip is to paint the outside of the box white to cut down on heat absorption.

Now for our sniffers. Here's a word about sweeteners, digesters, decomposers, odor-eaters — those products that rescue olfactory glands from the onerous fate of odiferous overdoses! First, what not to do.

Big Don't

Don't put toxic chemicals or formaldehyde-based additives into holding tanks. They interfere with the enzyme and bacterial action that is necessary for expedient decomposition. Sewage treatment plants recommend organic products.
There are a myriad of odor-controlling, pathogen-killing products on the market. I have picked two naturally derived formulas that are aromatic, sewage digestion enhancers.

Bio-Balance RM 41 ($3.88 for eight ounces or $9.67 for one quart and a sprayer, from Tri Synergy Inc., P.O. Box 27015, San Diego, CA 92198, phone 800-446-6076). Made of three strains of bacillus bacteria, RM-41 is a liquid sweetener/sewage digester that has been given a light Ivory Soap fragrance. Lisa Butler, co-founder of Tri Synergy, says RM-41 was originally developed at the request of several California State Parks for use in R.V. holding tanks. Butler explains that flies are attracted by the odor of feces. RM-41's perfume masks the odor until the bacteria can go to work. Buy it at some R.V. campgrounds or from Tri Synergy.

First Round Knock Out ($20 for one pint with a trigger sprayer, from Southwest Hollowell, 2140 East Fifth Street, Suite 9, Tempe, AZ 85281, phone 602-966-3988). Jim Hilleary, concocter of this magic eucalyptus potion, says, "It's the answer to every person's prayer — that their shit doesn't stink!" More significant is this report in a letter to Hilleary from a Grand Canyon boater: "Our river trip was ten days long with fourteen healthy kayakers, we treated our Porta Potti as you suggested at the beginning of the trip, it was four days later before we had to treat it again." Hilleary's product is a combination of natural botanical oils and odor-eating enzymes. Yours truly squirted some around her home (an old dairy barn with lots of interesting out-of-the-ordinary smells); I thought the fragrance reminiscent of the old cold remedy, Vicks VapoRub. A little goes a long way. First Round Knock Out also comes by the half case ($101.70 for six pints and one sprayer) and the full case ($203.40 for twelve pints and two sprayers).

◆

Since I first began writing about the wilderness disposal of solid bodily waste, the practice of packing-it-out has moved from rivers, up mountainsides, across deserts, and out onto oceans. The number of people willing to adopt or invent removal techniques is astounding. Also amazing is the technology growing up around it, which you will encounter further in Chapter Four. We are perhaps not far from a marketable sonic crap-zapper with the capacity to instantly alter the molecular structure of a human turd. Imagine! A Trekkie phaser gun for the mountain trekker. Poop and poof?

PLIGHT OF THE SOLO POOP PACKER

Everyone, at some time, is a continent of one.

Pico Iyer, *Falling Off the Map*

You cannot escape. Everyday a part of you turns to shit.

Don Sabbath and Mandel Hall,
End Product, The First Taboo

Now for a walk on the wild side. Admittedly, the concept of carting around warm poop in a backpack is not just revolutionary; at first thought, it's overwhelmingly repulsive. Only if you're lucky will the weather be cold enough to freeze it. To get past the involuntary "gak!" reaction, it helps to look upon the whole procedure as one of the marvels of physics — that shrinkage of food supply as the shit container fills — a perfect example of Einstein's $E = mc^2$. When we deal this intimately with our own volume of excrement, we cannot escape a firsthand, eye-opening reflection on the magical powers of Mother Nature.

Without further ado, we will consider the whens and hows of packing-it-out for the individual when hole-digging is impossible or non-ecological. Packing-it-out is recommended for rock climbers (those uncouth beasts); for campers venturing into severe weather conditions (when you can't locate any dirt or you'd rather stay in the tent); for visitors to high use areas in an effort to keep those places looking pristine; for all the untidy Himalayan litterbugs; and for sea kayakers and cavers or anyone visiting fragile ecosystems. Understandably, rock climbers have the toughest time given the added acrobatics involved in keeping the face of a mountain clean. What can I say? Practice. Select a container and hang off the patio tree.

Recent years have seen increasing demand for a viable inoffensive method for getting the fecal matter of individuals back to the trailhead. In different corners of the continent, inventive genius has been quietly at work, coming to the aid of the solo poop packer. It's a tricky bill to fill. A user-friendly design for the individual covers much the same territory as for the group, but the inventor must bear in mind the typical poop packer will probably be more of a twice-a-year hiker or sea kayaker, softer on flush apparatus than a paid river guide who's inured to Porta Potti duty. To start off, a container must be sturdy but lightweight, small enough to be convincingly carried, yet big enough to hold several days' deposits. It must have a positively reliable seal. No one wants this item coming open inside their backpack. It would also be lovely if it could vent gases so it would not to blow up inside a backpack. And it should not, when in use, easily (ever!) tip over. It should be user friendly to flush and sterilize, or else completely biodegradable. A shape convenient for direct deposit might be helpful. Other pluses would be compatibility with R.V. dumping stations and septic tanks.

For five years my friend Rick Spittler and I have been kicking around ideas and we think we finally have a prototype. We do! It's just that Rick claims it looks more like a bomb and says the FBI is following him around. "They're hard to convince," he moans, "that a person only shits in these things." Meanwhile, in all sincerity, I must confess I've managed to avoid our actual testing grounds. It is Rick's garage that is full of containers of every conceivable shape, size, and material; they line the shelves on three walls, each has a label, a date, an explanation of the experiment, some are packaged with enzymes, some in paper, some in cellulose, the bigger containers stuffed with a week's accumulation, just to see if they fit. The other day his four-year-old son wandered into the garage and asked, "Dad? What's in these bags? It looks like poop!" Four states away, my job is to console Rick over the phone. I always try to be helpful. "Just tell that kid what's in those bags is his college education."

Getting to the nuts and bolts, we've christened our bomb **Go With the J-UHG** ($34.50 from Go With the J-UGH, P.O. Box 352, Stevensville, MT 59870, phone 800-642-JUGH). At the time of conception, this name suited our sentiments — now we sit around waiting to be sued by someone who has a *real* jug, full of something like four-hundred-year-old whiskey. Our J-UGH is a lightweight (eighteen ounces) aluminum cylinder (3" diameter). The *Sojourner* model (15" length) will hold three to six deposits with accompanying t.p., largely depending on an individual's eating habits — are you a butterfly, pink flamingo, or Jurassic diplodocus? — and the amount of tissue required. The shorter *Sprinter* (10" length) is recommended for day or overnight trips. Deposits are made easily, and almost anywhere, onto a square of absorbent paper (paper towel will work) and then transferred into the cylinder. Wrappings help with aesthetics and with post trip cleaning; in most cases, the individual packages pop out neatly one at a time leaving little to clean. When it comes to dumping, both ends of the cylinder are fitted with removable screw-on lids (with gaskets), allowing for the content's expedient exit and easy access for cleaning. The contents are acceptable in sewers, septic tanks, vault-type outhouses, even home toilets when several flushes are employed. Further cleaning can be accomplished with the help of a bottle brush. During testing, a packed cylinder absorbed two days of direct California sun and never blew its lids. Custom lengths can be made to order. The J-UGH is designed for the high country hiker, backcountry skier, sea kayaker, mountain climber, hunter . . . even the cross-country cyclist and four-wheeler.

From Canada comes our competition and possibly the salvation of the planet. It's the **Personal Biodegradable Wilderness Toilet** (approximately $2; from David Cormier, 86 Edgeview Drive NW, Calgary, Alberta, Canada, phone 403-547-0933). David Cormier, avid hiker, rock climber, and student of industrial design at the University of Calgary, is intent on developing a "scat sack" with a disappearing act that's capable of rendering its contents pathogen-free within several days. The sack is to be made from a new generation of biodegradable polymers (not dependent on ultraviolet light for decomposition) and designed to disintegrate completely in six months. It's meant to be a *one person/one use unit*, sealing permanently after direct deposit. To operate, one holds it by both hands in a full or partial squat (some support for the buttocks is assumed in the partial squat). The sack could be set down during wiping, as a special absorbent layer would immediately capture any liquid. Cormier's intent is for each sack to have a microporous patch that will vent gases without leaking liquid. A package of ten, weighing approximately one pound, would be as big as a box of one hundred facial tissues. A waterproof haul sack could be used for transporting several days' bags. Disposal options range from wilderness burial to composting or passing it through some sort of grinder. At backcountry trailheads, a mobile holding tank might serve as a collecting station, or a rotating vault system could be the repository — the full tanks would be ready to pump six months after closing. With wilderness burial, the advantage over using the cat hole method burial is that harmful pathogens wouldn't be hanging around in the soil for a year. Cormier plans to proceed with a prototype and testing. By the time you read this paragraph, with any luck he will have a million scat sacks for sale.

The high Sierras gives us the *poop tube*. The National Park Service (NPS) now advocates packing-it-out on the climbing routes in Yosemite National Park (by other means than the traditional flinging of laden paper bags into the cosmos). Enter poop tubes! Mark Butler is a climber and a physical science specialist with NPS, and though he refuses to make any claims on the poop tube's design, he uses one and promotes them as inexpensive do-it-yourself containers for packing-it-out. Construction is easy and materials are readily available in most hardware stores across

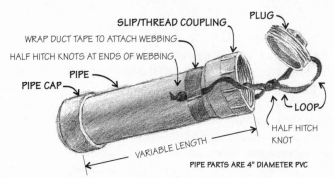

SLIP/THREAD COUPLING
PLUG
WRAP DUCT TAPE TO ATTACH WEBBING
HALF HITCH KNOTS AT ENDS OF WEBBING
PIPE
PIPE CAP
LOOP
HALF HITCH KNOT
VARIABLE LENGTH
PIPE PARTS ARE 4" DIAMETER PVC

the country. Simply cut a piece of PVC pipe (4" diameter) to the length of your trip, so to speak, twelve to twenty-five inches. Glue a cap on one end and buy a plug for the other. With super tape (climber's webbing) and a little duct tape, Butler slings the tube from the bottom of his haul sack (see illustration). Deposits are made into brown paper bags containing a bit of kitty litter and then dropped into the tube. At the end of a trip, the contents are conveniently dumped into one of the park's vault toilets.

For the adventurer willing to leave behind western civilization's characteristic prudishness, there are more home-grown ways of coping (and I don't mean enemas). Inexpensive household containers have been expropriated for outdoor use on many occasions. I have reports of Tupperware salad bowls being used by backpackers, two people to a bowl in some cases. (I couldn't help wondering if this type of sharing cements relationships in the same way that showering together does during a drought.) One flaw in the Tupperware system involves methane build-up: a morning's hike under a hot sun will invariably pop the seal. But people seem to manage by being attentive. A Tupperware bowl (or bowl of similar design) is also the favorite of Karen Stimpson, trail keeper for the Maine Island Trail. She started out by adding a handful of kitty litter, but has now progressed to rolling her deposit in a bit of sand, earth, or dried leaves before scooping it up. "The container cleans easier," she says. Surely this is all new testimony to the function of Tupperware. (I wonder if the Tupperware folks know?) If you don't own any of their dandy containers, you can always fall back on the elemental milk carton with duct tape, the contents to be emptied down a toilet and the carton itself washed before discarding. When using kitty litter, buy the cheapest available, as it's usually straight betonite, a powdery clay soil.

Once again, if like me, you lack expertise with gravity, here are a few hints on solitary collecting. In snow, scoop out a small hole and tuck your container into it (this would work better with Tupperware or scat sacks than paper collectors). Then sit down. If it's too cold, carefully rest your buns upon your gloves. If you have the leisure and inclination, you can build a royal throne, a chair-high mound with the container hole in the top. In inclement weather, turn your container into a chamber pot inside your tent. This will be a breeze provided you know your fellow campers well. If you are desperate enough, who cares? Better yet, send *them* into the blizzard. Sometimes kneeling can be an alternative to squatting. Straddle your container with your knees somewhat apart and your heels farther apart, in a comfortable position. With your task completed, tuck the packaged results into a snow bank until morning.

Other cosmic means of disposal helpful to the individual are under contemplation — one with only a few kinks to be worked out. I met a man who is dreaming up a system for on-site incineration to dehydrate and sterilize feces at each night's camp. When I saw him last, he was calculating how much fuel he needed to be pack along. Also there are rumors, however untraceable, about a biodegradable bag made out of cheese.

Already perfected and coming into their day for backcountry use are solar composting toilets, which alleviate the poop packer's task completely. Though prohibited in designated wilderness areas where the building of permanent structures is prohibited, they are seen as a godsend in many places. In the Broken Group Islands in Barkley Sound, British Columbia — a sea kayaker's haven from the relentless Pacific Ocean — solar composting toilets ease the headache of human waste management for boaters and the Pacific Rim National Park. Hired to erect Phoenix Composting Toilets, the folks at Sunergy in Cremona, Alberta, proved they are not just wilderness plumbers, but also installation artists. Using coastline flotsam for a driftwood rafter here, a driftwood railing there, fanciful coat hooks and shelving, seashell collages for wall decor, and a natural sweep to ramps and stairs, they created whimsical, inviting shelters that seem in turn to elicit better care from their frequenters. The Canada Park Service reports the solar composting toilets entail less maintenance than legendary pit toilets, which required moving twice a year. And everyone agrees, the aroma is far sweeter. With the ventilating fan, the little abodes ares virtually odorless.

In the state of Washington, the solar composting toilet offers opportunity for corporate advertising, tax write-offs for the financially flush, or even dubious means to immortality. Sandie Nelson jokes that her major job as executive director of Washington Water Trails has been to create a potty fund for the Cascadia Marine Trail, a string of island campsites. The trail is designated accessible for only "human- or wind-powered, small, beachable crafts." An individual or company willing to spring the $3,000 to $5,000 donation required for installation will see their name gracing a plaque over the outhouse door — much in the manner that engraved brass plates honor the donors of theater seats. Cascade Designs, maker of Therma-a-REST sleeping pads, is first in line for sponsorship. Hurry, hurry, hurry — there won't be enough for everybody! Call Washington Water Trails at 206-545-9161.

Yet another solution, and maybe not as far-fetched as it sounds, runs along the idea of carrying your own biodegrader: a batch of beetles, earthworms, or bacteria that neutralize noxious odors and turn excrement into earth. One woman wrote to me about putting scarab beetles — descendants of the ancient Egyptian dung beetles — to work in her pit toilet. She's even successfully wintered them over. Another woman suggested treatment plants with earthworms instead of water sewer systems. Brilliant! was my first thought upon hearing their ideas. Let's roll back in time to when collected night soils fertilized crops — as recently as the early 1800s here in the United States. My enthusiasm was fueled in part by having just completed Latee Fahm's *The Waste of Nations*, a study, to my mind, that should be required reading for anyone planning to be around for the twenty-first century. Clearly, our direction should be toward simplicity, the elimination of toxic processes, and the adoption of systems that are economically sound in the overall planet's cycle of food-to-feces-to-fertilizer-to-food. But for the backpacker or the sea kayaker, two questions came to mind: how could this work on the trail and what are the environmental consequences of turning scarab beetles loose all over the high country? Please keep me informed.

Completely in another realm, comes a new, if unconventional, technique for disposing of human waste — specifically for remote, low use wilderness areas. Revolutionary in both terminology and approach, this method emerged in the last few years from the prominent outdoor schools. At Cal Adventures, University of California at Berkeley, is the practice of (get ready!) *frosting a rock*. At Colorado Outward Bound and the National Outdoor Leadership School in Wyoming, the same procedure is called, yet more graphically, *smearing*. A hiker rises from an afternoon nap, takes in a panoramic sweep of mountain pinnacles, languidly stretches, and then proclaims to all present, "I think I have to go frost a rock."

At first acquaintance, one might think the whole idea invented by pre-schoolers, and possibly child's play is what sparked the cranial gears of some cruiser of rugged terrain. No one's owning up! Though the word gross first comes to mind, in actuality, what's required to properly execute this technique is a finely honed sense of aesthetics and a well-schooled background in both climate and terrain. This is not a matter for the timid or the tyro.

With correct backcountry conditions, frosting a rock can be the most practical and refreshingly elemental method of disposal for trekker and our weary old Mother. But it can only be employed strictly in limited circumstances. Four elements must be present before considering its use: a remote location, intense sunlight, a dry season, and lack of a well-developed soil (no bacterial activity or no soil). This suggests your travel is above timberline, through blazing sand or hardpan deserts, across extensive boulder fields, scree, or lava flows, or over vast expanses of tundra in subzero climates where the ground is continuously frozen. If you are not in a dry climate, it must be a dry season with no chance of fecal matter being carried away by storm runoff or buried beneath snow drifts to thaw in the spring. In effect, you are employing the sewage treatment plant of the heavens, the almighty solar incinerator: ultraviolet rays bake pathogens and dehydrate your leavings until wind carries off the final parched flakes.

Remoteness is a major consideration. It's not cricket to ruin the next person's well-deserved sojourn through pristine vistas. If an area is likely to receive visitors within two weeks of your passing, you should be packing-it-out, not frosting. It is possible, however, to decrease the likelihood of someone encountering your signature (of sorts) by avoiding world-class attractions. Get off and away from a sculpted boulder garden where people might tend to loll after lunch. Instead of climbing on top of a boulder, pick out a square foot of flat rock and cart it off to where the view isn't quite so inspiring.

This brings us to actual procedure. With sun the prime factor in decomposition, select a spot that catches daylong direct light. Your spatula will be a handy stone. First, you shit on the rock. Then frost the side of the rock that receives optimum sun. Frost as thinly as possible, leaving the stone alongside, also turned up to the sun. When I asked my Cal Adventures instructor, "Just how thin are we talking here?" the answer came, of course, "Pretend you're frosting a cake!" If midway into your plastering job, you begin to come a little unstuck, try viewing it as an art form or just another in the long list of miracles given us by the sun gods, Helios and Apollo.

◆

Our wild lands shrink, our urban lifestyles manufacture more madness, and our need to touch nature increases. More overuse is directly ahead of us. It's easy to see in the simple arithmetic of numbers of one-sit holes that packing-it-out will expand the limits of visitation in high use areas. Misuse on top of overuse further narrows the territory of enjoyable wild terrain. In essence, a shrinking wilderness means more warm poop in your backpack! (A little something to remember the next time your vote is needed for preservation.)

We can wend earth's curves from sheer rock faces to sea-shore marshes in the company of good friends, but one act will remain solitary: shitting. In learning to be a poop packer, if you begin to feel a little queasy, take comfort in the thought that you won't, in fact, be alone — either in the feeling or in pack-ing-it-out. Trust me, the *individual* Porta Potti is the backwoods tsunami of the future and a small price to pay for preserving solitudinous acreage. Grab your container. Hold your nose, if it helps. And take your shit with you when you leave.

McVey '89

TREKKER'S TROTS

Lomotil, lomotil, wherefore art thou,
my lomotil?

Anonymous traveler in Puerto Vallarta

During the violent shaking of an earthquake, a solid, earth-filled dam can turn into liquid and wash away. Trekker's trots is a similar phenomenon occurring within the intestinal walls of the mammalian body. I've seen it happen to my Clydesdales during Fourth of July fireworks celebrations at the country fair. Seconds after the first cannon blasts, the horses are dispersing streams of green alfalfa soup. When this instantaneous liquefaction happens in the species *Homo sapiens*, we call it: *turista*, *Montezuma's revenge*, the *green apple two-step*, or, quite simply, the *shits*.

Such a watery biological response can be brought about by any number of things in addition to flus and intestinal diseases. Our immune systems grow up where we do, leaving our resistances unequipped for various foreign foods and water. Traveling itself can be overwhelming; changes in climate, altitude, and time zone all take their toll on the human system. Anxiety about making all (or missing half) your travel connections can have anyone reaching for Riopan Plus or Kaopectate. The sheer fright of an adventure a bit too thrilling can "set it off" faster than a shaken beer exits its container. Two of my favorite friends seem to be hit by this particular disorder whenever they set foot inside an airport; thus, they have coined another modern euphemism, 'air-porters,' for that most dreaded of afflictions, traveler's diarrhea.

This short chapter — short as I hope all your bouts with this subject will be — emphasizes prevention. Once you've been struck by an airporter, there isn't a whole lot to be said — only to resist cleaning up in a nearby creek and remember to do any washing above the high water line. It helps to have a good friend, someone to bring you wash water and clothes and offer comfort. Someone who won't hold their sides and laugh at your condition.

Focusing on prevention automatically brings us face to face with sanitation practices. Since enteric pathogens (the intestinal bad guys) are transmitted by various forms of fecal-oral contact, logically, then, the first step toward prevention is to ritualize hand washing. Get yourself and all your traveling companions into the habit of washing *after* squatting and *before* preparing food or eating. Be neurotic about it! At each camp on a commercial river trip, guides set up a bucket of water, a bar of soap, and a cup or long-handled ladle near the group Porta Potti. The ladle is for scooping water out of the bucket, so you don't contaminate the clean water by thrusting your hands into it.

Another excellent washing system, the *refried bean wash*, was invented by my cohort in the study of backcountry human waste management, Dan Ritzman. The idea sprung from traditional fare in camp cooking: Rosarita refried beans, pork and beans, hot chili beans, bean pot stew — there's always a bean can around. The bigger the can, the longer the wash. Punch two holes opposite each other and near the top rim of an empty, well-scrubbed bean can and tie a string or piece of wire between them, making a bucket-like handle. Punch another small hole in the can's side near the bottom. Dunk it into your fresh water bucket, to fill, and through the bottom hole it will produce a steady stream for soaping and rinsing. Dan sets it at the front edge of a flat-topped boulder or hangs it in a tree.

If you're traveling in your own group without a Porta Potti, you can set up a washing arrangement at the edge of camp in the area where you station the shovel, toilet paper, and refuse bag. I can't stress enough the importance of hand washing for outdoor people who tend to equate ruggedness — that messing and sweating about in earth's fresh fragrant dirt — with the *primeval*, the long sought-after excuse not to bathe for days.

Another precaution against the shits is to watch what you eat and drink. Properly refrigerate perishable foods and carefully disinfect all drinking, cooking, food washing, and hand washing water. The treatment of wilderness water against infectious organisms is termed *field water disinfection*. This is defined as "removing or destroying harmful microorganisms" in an article by Dr. Howard Backer, M.D., entitled "Field Water Disinfection" published in *Management of Wilderness and Environmental Emergenices*, 1994 edition, edited by Auerbach and Geehr (St. Louis, Baltimore, Toronto: C.V. Mosby). Backer tells us disinfection should not be confused with sterilization which is "the destruction or removal of all life forms" and "not necessary, since not all organisms are enteric human pathogens." The term "purification" that shows up frequently in product literature, has a broad range of interpretation. According to Backer, it technically means "the removal of organic or inorganic chemicals and particulate matter, including radioactive particles. While purification can eliminate offensive color, taste, and odor, it may not remove or kill microorganisms." To be perfectly clear, you should ask the manufacturer for a definition.

Enteric pathogens come in three categories: parasitic organisms, bacteria, and viruses. In the first category, the protozoan cysts of *Giardia* and oocysts of *Cryptosporidium* are widespread in wilderness water and must be considered a hazard everywhere in the world. In the United States and Canada, problematic bacteria cannot be called epidemic, but they turn up occasionally and seem to be on the increase. In other parts of the world, particularly in developing countries, field water and even municipal water supplies must be treated for protozoan cysts, bacteria, and most importantly, for viruses.

There are any number of filtration systems on the market — some gravity feed, some pumps — that will effectively remove protozoan cysts. To varying degrees, the same systems will remove bacteria. A filter with an "absolute" pore size of 3.0 microns will remove *Giardia* and *Cryptosporidium*; a filter of 0.2 microns will also eliminate all bacteria ("absolute" means no organism bigger than the size of the hole can pass through).

The disinfecting process for viruses is much different. A filter with a pore size fine enough to strain viruses out would be too difficult to push water through. Acceptable choices for virus disinfecting employ some form of iodine or chlorine. What is good for killing viruses, however, does not always work on protozoan cysts. Boiling will kill everything but it also has drawbacks. At the time of this writing, there are several systems available that will effectively disinfect for all enteric pathogens (protozoan cysts, bacteria, and viruses): three of the PUR pump/filters, the General Ecology Microlite and First Need Trav-L-Pure that come with iodine tablets, the Penta-Pure Oasis, the PentaPure Water Jug, and according to their literature, the Pocket Travel Well and Trekker Travel Well.

If you're headed into the United States or Canadian interior, you need nothing more than a simple mechanical filter to remove protozoan cysts and bacteria. Some are fashioned as hand or foot pumps, others are slower gravity feed systems. Many have prefilters that capture larger debris and sediment that serve to extend the life of a filter. Some are designed to back-flush to unclog. With others, you will be able to remove particles by brushing the filter's outer surface. Ceramic filters have the longest life and are easily cleaned by scrubbing. Become familiar with replacement filter costs because eventually all filters need to be changed. If you purchase an activated carbon filter, it will also remove organic chemicals such as herbicides, pesticides, diesel fuel, solvents, and fertilizers. On the down side, carbon filters must be replaced regularly, regardless of whether they are clogged. They collect material by the process of *adsorption* (the clinging of molecules to a solid surface) and when surface limits are reached, previously adsorbed materials begin to be released. The difficulty is in knowing just when this releasing begins. Andreas King, assistant editor of *Waste & Water Treatment Journal*, London, England, expresses great skepticism about manufacturers' claims and states that common testing has shown that "breakthrough" occurs with most activated carbon filters after less than fifty gallons.

It's advantageous to have a unit that can be easily disassembled for cleaning and repairing in the field — some require the skill of an arthroscopic surgeon. Ask for a demonstration. It's also wise to simulate field pumping before plunking down your money — the smooth operation of certain models comes only with prior apprenticeship to a contortionist, extra limbs, or the assistance of a second person.

I've heard it said if you want reliable information from a manufacturer, read the advertising and divide by ten. Good drinking water is serious business: approach with caution any items which ring of fads or resemble toys. Read the fine print, ask questions, be satisfied.

You will not be able to find a perfect filter: there are none. No filter can protect you one hundred percent. Choose one that will fit your lifestyle and the places you plan to visit. Are you an avid day hiker, or a mountain peak to pinnacle nut? Are you organizing the Eastern States Stamp Collectors Club for a week-long excursion into fresh air? Are you off to Africa? Or are you a lone Montana hunter shoeing the old horse for the fall run up the mountainside?

Here follows a bit of information about various filters. I have focused mainly on outfits that would fill the needs of solo, pair, or small group (three to four) travelers. And though I haven't conducted any scientific studies, neither have I presented systems whose reliability seemed overly dubious. Please keep in mind that specifications are taken from the manufacturers' claims; as yet, there are no set standards for regulating or testing. The Environmental Protection Agency, when you call their drinking water hot line (800-426-4791), will say they do not have set standards for field water disinfecting systems. The EPA does not approve or endorse field water filtration units as such. At this time, products with an EPA registration number have merely been registered as a pesticide that has been tested and found not to cause "harmful health effects."

Ceramic filters are sometimes impregnated with silver, which will act as a bactericide (kills bacteria) or be bacteriostatic (prevent further growth of bacteria). With all filters, housings should be regularly examined for cracks that can be a cause of contamination. Filter capabilities — generally given in gallons, as the life of a filter — will fluctuate greatly on the downside when filtering muddy, debris-laden, or glacial water; or when your apparatus is partially clogged; or when Sasquatch has planted a big foot on your hose.

Katadyn Pocket Filter ($250; replacement filter $150; weighs 23 oz.; output 1.3 pints/minute; pore size 0.2 microns; capacity unlimited; from Katadyn USA, 3020 N. Scottsdale Road, Scottsdale, AZ 85251, phone 800-950-0808). For forty years the Swiss-made Katadyns with their easily cleaned ceramic elements have been known as the Mercedes of filters, costing far more but lasting much longer. I have a friend who has pushed one to its limits for six years. Katadyn ceramic is impregnated with the silver that inhibits bacterial growth. Its mechanical straining system will take out protozoan cysts and all bacteria. For the outdoor enthusiast putting miles on a filter every week, the Katadyns have been the long-standing best choice. (Times are changing rapidly now in the water treatment field, and Katadyn is meeting stiff competition in the marketplace. Several less expensive filters are lighter in weight and more efficient, and have all sorts of bells and whistles. There are less expensive ceramic designs as well.) The **Mini Katadyn** ($150; replacement filter $70; weighs 8 oz.; output 0.7 pints/minute; pore size 0.2 microns; capacity 650 to 2,000 gallons) has the same ceramic filter in a smaller package. The *Backpacker* (June 1992) review of filters called it "the easiest-cleaning filter available, one that lasts just about forever." Keep in mind the Mini's capacity when considering other comparably sized mechanical filters. The **Expedition Katadyn** ($725; replacement filter $80; weighs 12 lbs.; output 8.0 pints/minute; pore size 0.2 microns; capacity 10,000 to 15,000 gallons) is the largest of their pump filters, a good choice for groups or outfitters. Katadyn also has a gravity feed **Syphon** ($85; replacement filter $80; weighs 32 oz.; output 0.33 pints/minute; pore size 0.2 microns; capacity unlimited) and the larger **TRK-Dripfilter** ($250; replacement filter $160; weighs 11 lbs.; output 10 gallons/day; pore size 0.2 microns; capacity unlimited). Katadyn receives calls from people who have used the same Syphon or TRK-Dripfilter successfully in the bush for ten to fifteen years, and from others who report being on their third generation using the same Pocket Filter.

MSR WaterWorks ($125; membrane replacement filter $32; carbon replacement filter $20; weighs 17.5 oz.; output 2.0 pints/minute; pore size 0.2 microns; from Mountain Safety Research, P.O. Box 24547, Seattle, WA 98134, phone 800-877-9MSR). This is the original MSR, a four filter system. On the end of the intake hose is a weighted filter (85 microns) with a float for keeping it off a river bottom, adjustable for different depths. In-line in the hose is another prefilter screen, made of stainless steel, which can be cleaned with Efferdent dental tablets or hydrogen peroxide. A carbon filter removes organic chemicals, and a membrane filter (0.2 microns) mechanically takes out protozoan cysts and bacteria. The pivot-action handles of the MSR are reminiscent of the old well pump, operating ergonomically to push water through the multi-filter system. The housing's threaded base attaches directly to a standard poly bottle or one of MSR's collapsible *Dromedary* drink bags. This unit is known for simple field maintenance and, unfortunately, for its tendency to clog quickly. **MSR WaterWorks Ceramic** ($140; membrane replacement filter $32; ceramic replacement filter $30; weighs 17 oz.; output 2.0 pints/minute; pore size 0.2 microns). The new 1994 model, outfitted with a ceramic prefilter of 0.6 microns, will be a popular filter. The ceramic is fired in such a way as to produce carbon throughout. It functions in the same manner as an activated carbon filter, removing organic chemicals, while greatly extending the unclogged life of the membrane filter. You may have noticed there are no gallon capacities listed for these filters. The MSR folks feel it's almost unethical to make definitive statements about longevity when there are so many variables. This is not sleeping bag ratings they say, this is drinking water we're talking about. Bravo!

Relags Travel Filter ($149.95; replacement filter $75; weighs 21 oz.; output 1.4 pints/minute; pore size 0.5 microns; capacity 3,500 to 5,000 gallons; from Relags USA, Inc., 1705 14th Street, Suite 119, Boulder, CO 80302, phone 303-440-8047). This one is a German-made filter (similar to the Katadyn) that has recently become available in the United States. It has an easy to clean, long life ceramic filter. It is not impregnated with silver but can be boiled to sterilize before going on a trip. The housing is made of a material called NORYL, a resin that will survive cold temperatures or dropping, without cracking. The Relags disinfects for parasitic organisms and most bacteria.

Basic Designs Ceramic Filter Pump ($29.95; replacement filter $14.99; weighs 8 oz.; output 1.0 pint/ minute; pore size 0.9 microns; capacity up to 500 gallons; from Basic Designs, Inc.,

335 A O'Hair Court, Santa Rosa, CA 95407, phone 707-575-1220). This is a ceramic filter impregnated with bacteriostatic silver. The intake hose is fitted with a prefilter foam boot (200 microns) of polyurethane, and the output hose has a clip for attaching to a canteen or the pot you are pumping into. This unit disinfects for parasitic organisms and most bacteria. Concerned about the 0.9 microns and the possibility of small bacteria swimming through, I spoke with David Webb, a water filtration expert working for Royal Doulton Water Filters, the English manufacturers of the Basic Designs ceramic component. Webb explains that a tortuous labyrinth in the ceramic — millions and millions of sub-micron pores that water must travel through before being pumped into your glass — is responsible for capturing bacteria smaller than the absolute pore size. For organisms of 0.1 microns Basic Designs filters have tested 99.7 percent effective in eliminating harmful bacteria. Henry Doulton (same family as Royal Doulton Bone China) began making filters in 1827 and the first Doulton ceramic filter was produced in 1901. Soon after the turn of the century, Queen Victoria, worried about cholera epidemics and the plethora of feces bobbing down the Thames, bestowed a Royal Warrant upon the Doulton filters (meaning royalty likes them and buys them!). The *High-Flow Ceramic* ($79.99; replacement filter $44.99; weighs 24 oz.; output 0.5 pint/minute; pore size 0.9 microns; capacity 1,000 gallons) is a gravity feed system with a silver impregnated ceramic filter. Carbon inside the ceramic will remove organic chemicals. Hang up the reservoir in camp, go for an afternoon's hike, and when you return you have seven quarts of drinkable water. The manufacturers say this system is idiot-proof and also field serviceable by brushing the cartridge with the cleaning pad that is provided.

First Need Delux ($59.95; replacement filter $28.95; weighs 15 oz.; output 2.0 pints/minute; pore size 0.4 microns; capacity 100 gallons; from General Ecology, Inc., 151 Sheree Boulevard, Exton, PA 19341, phone 800-441-8166). The Delux is GE's new improved model, easier to operate than their infamous Original, because the canister is attached to the pump. Chip Umsted, marketing manager, says the mechanical depth filter with activated carbon "works like a fly trying to get through a screen three-quarters of an inch thick." Protozoan cysts are stopped on the outside, bacteria is trapped in the first few millimeters, and organic chemicals — herbicides, pesticides, PCBs, TCE (trichloroethelyne) — are collected further inside. Umsted claims there is not a problem with releasing already adsorbed material; he says the cartridges will clog long before the capacity of the activated carbon is used up. With this filter, unclogging is accomplished by back flushing. An optional prefilter (10 microns) and bottle-filler cap, which will screw onto wide-mouthed trail bottles, are packaged together for $8.95. The **First Need Original** ($48.95; replacement filter $28.95; weighs 13 oz.; output 1.5 pints/minute; pore size 0.4 microns; capacity 100 gallons) has the same filter cartridge as the Delux. The Original is the apparatus disparaged by many as needing more arms and feet to operate than the average person comes equipped with at birth. Using it with the optional prefilter and bottle-filler cap offered with the Delux makes it a little handier to operate. The **General Ecology Microlite** ($29.95; replacement filter 2/$9.95; weighs 7 oz.; output 1+ pints/minute; pore size 0.5 microns; capacity 15 gallons) is said to disinfect for all enteric pathogens, even viruses, as included in the price is a package of iodine tablets, Potable Aqua. Treat water with the iodine first, then pump it through the filter to remove protozoa and improve the taste. This is the same mechanical depth filter with activated carbon described in the Delux. The Microlite's intake hose stores conveniently underneath the handle. On the housing bottom, there's a removable (3" diameter) rubber cap that covers a nesting of built-in bottle tops. This allows you to screw the pump directly onto wide-mouthed trail bottles, snap it onto most bike bottles (or squeeze bottles), or rest it on narrow-mouthed pop bottles. The **First Need Trav-L-Pure** ($119.95; replacement filter $29.95; weighs 22 oz.; output 1.5 pints/minute; pore size 0.4 microns; capacity 100 gallons) is a little black box (no hoses), touted by the manufacturer as the "civilized filter" because you can set it unobtrusively on your dinner table in a questionable restaurant and it will treat all the water that's served you. The Trav-L-Pure has the same filter as the other First Need products. Like the Microlite, it comes with Potable Aqua tablets. A built-in reservoir (22 ounce capacity) accepts tap water, or you can dunk the whole thing into a stream to fill it. Pop a tablet into the reservoir and then pump it through as you need it. Two self-contained prefilters (10 microns and 5 microns) extend the life of the filter. *First Need Base Camp* ($449.95; replacement filter $59.95; weighs 4 lbs.; output 8 pints/minute; pore size 0.4 microns; capacity 500 gallons). The Base Camp is fairly self-explanatory; once again, it has the same filter cartridge. A 10 micron prefilter is included.

SweetWater Guardian ($49.95; replacement filter $19.95; weighs 11 oz.; output 2.0 pints/minute; pore size 0.2 microns; capacity 200 gallons; from SweetWater Inc., 4725 Nautilus Court South, Suite #3, Boulder, CO 80301, phone 800-55SWEET). If you walk into The Trailhead outdoor store in Missoula, Montana, and talk to Clara McClane, you will find she's clearly enamored of the new SweetWater. First she makes certain you note the outfit's price. Then she points to the ingeniously designed prefilter on the intake — shaped somewhat like a squat-bowled tobacco pipe, topped with a one hundred micron screen, and weighted, which taken altogether enables it to rest directly on a stream bed without sucking in silt. You begin to browse the brochure she has thrust at you and are thinking of asking to see the other prefilter — the optional four-micron — called the *Silt Stopper* ($7.95), but Clara is deftly guiding the entire be-hosed apparatus into your hands, politely pressing you to try the lever action pump handle. She praises it as a system that doesn't entail a person's being born with three arms to operate. "Look at this!" she says, turning over the end of the output hose. You peer into a series of bottle tops nested inside each other, designed to fit containers of various neck sizes. Then there's the overall featherweight — she's gently bouncing it off her upturned palms. And the easy dismantling for field maintenance — she's got it apart on the counter top. Ask about the disinfecting properties and Clara explains it's a depth filter with carbon that will remove protozoan cysts, bacteria, and organic chemicals. Lastly, Clara impresses upon you the wisdom of a recyclable filter cartridge and she shows you the return envelope that SweetWater supplies every buyer (recycling saves you $2.00 on a replacement cartridge). When I left the store, I had one under my arm — either because SweetWater is a great filter or Clara was my granny's name.

Timberline ($24.95; replacement filter $12.95; weighs 6 oz.; output 1.8 pints/minute; pore size 2.0 microns; capacity 50 gallons; from Timberline Filter, P.O. Box 3435, Boulder, CO

80307, phone 303-440-8779). There are people who continue to swear by this simple economically priced filter — a glass-fiber/polyethylene matrix — capable of removing hippos, tree branches, and protozoan cysts from wilderness water. The outfit is surprisingly sturdy for its appearance. When it becomes plugged, the hand pump can either be back flushed or the filter replaced. If your excursions into the woods are only occasional and in the high country where problematic bacteria is not prolific, this is a filter that's easy on the pocketbook. Timberland in Canada is marketed under the name **Coghlan** (Coghlan's Ltd., Winnipeg, Manitoba R3T 4C7 Canada, phone 204-284-9550). Timberline is sold through discount stores and through the Campmor Catalog. The **Timberline Base Camp** ($50; replacement filter $20; weighs 11 oz.; output 2.0 pints/minute; pore size 2.0 microns; capacity 50 gallons) is a high-flow, two-gallon gravity feed reservoir made of coated nylon. The filter is the same as the hand pump's, only larger.

◆

If you are traveling to developing countries where sanitation is poor and hotel water supplies are questionable, you will need further protection — from viruses. The oldest method of disinfecting for viruses is simply **boiling**. Contrary to previous thinking, boiling is now thought to kill all waterborne enteric pathogens immediately. This is documented in the previously mentioned article, "Field Water Disinfection" by Dr. Howard Backer. He reports that any water is adequately disinfected by the time it reaches the boiling point — even at altitudes of 24,000 feet where the boiling point is as low as 74.5°C. The major problem with relying solely on boiling for disinfection is in lugging around enough fuel to accomplish the job.

The chemical disinfectants, **chlorine** and **iodine** (called halogens), are the other choices for eliminating viruses. Chlorine has long been the preferred disinfectant for municipal water supplies and iodine has been used by the military since the beginning of the century. Though halogens work well on viruses and bacteria, parasitic organisms have a resistance to them. Cryptosporidium, in particular, is highly resistant to chlorine. If you use either chemical to kill bacteria and viruses, take the added precaution of filter/disinfecting for parasitic organisms prior to the halogenating.

The average backcountry traveler is confronted with a confusing array of halogen forms. They come as chlorine tablets, ordinary household liquid bleach, iodine crystals, tincture of iodine, and iodine tablets. There are several things to consider when using these products. The stability of tablets is sometimes questionable; always buy a new bottle before each trip and keep it tightly sealed and out of the heat. You must be mindful of the corrosive effects of halogens, particularly of carelessly handled iodine crystals. Halogens do not disinfect properly when prepared in insufficient concentrations or without allowing adequate contact time. High pH, colder water temperatures, and cloudy water all decrease effectiveness. It's even possible for various organic and inorganic contaminants in water to combine chemically with a halogen and decrease a carefully measured out concentration.

Finally, when you have beautifully disinfected water, there is the not so beautiful chemical taste. You can help this situation in several ways. When treating cloudy water, prefilter through cheesecloth or a coffee paper, or allow it to settle in a bucket overnight. Demand for halogen is reduced by prefiltering, using warmer water, and allowing a longer contact time. Less halogen means better taste. Some people seem to adapt easily to drinking iodine water (I always think they have flavor-impaired taste buds). They're happy disguising the vapors with lemonade crystals or Tang. But I don't care what they say, this is when a carbon filter is worth triple its weight in my pack. The PUR iodine pump/filters are an excellent solution when you need virus protection. Mechanically, they strain out parasitic organisms; chemically, they kill bacteria and viruses; and with their optional carbon filter — all in one whoosh of the handle — they will supply saporous liquid for the discerning thirster. Hurrah!

A few medical cautions are to be observed with iodine: Do not use iodine when pregnant or if you have iodine sensitivity or thyroid disease. Iodine alters the results of thyroid functioning tests.

The following products are designed to annihilate viruses. **Polar Pure** ($8.95 to $12.50; capacity 500 gallons, from Polar Equipment, 12881 Foothill Lane, Saratoga, CA 95070, phone 408-867-4676) is a bottle of iodine crystals with a neat little trap to safely contain them. A thermometer on the side of the bottle tells you what the dosage should be. Accompanying literature informs us that iodine is only an odor, sensed in the nose and not on the tongue. When you run out of instant cherry drink, try pinching your nose. Polar Pure is long-lasting and not affected by age or exposure to air.

Potable Aqua ($3.95 to $5.95, capacity 12.5 gallons; from Wisconsin Pharmacal Co., Inc., One Repel Road, Jackson, WI 53037, phone 414-677-4121) is a bottle of fifty iodine tablets. One tablet will treat a quart of water in three minutes. If the water is turbid or extremely cold it takes two tablets and twenty minutes. Bring a magnifying glass to read the instructions. **Potable Aqua Plus** (50 tablets) is an iodine neutralizer packaged with Potable Aqua for a two step application. It converts iodine into a flavorless, odorless iodide. The active ingredient in the chemical change is ascorbic acid, or vitamin C. Sold together for $6.95 to $8.95.

PUR Scout ($64.95; replacement filter $34.95; weighs 12 oz.; output 2.0 pints/minute; pore size 1.0 microns; capacity 200 gallons; from PUR, 2229 Edgewood Avenue S., Minneapolis, MN 55426, phone 800-845-PURE). The PUR Scout, Explorer, and Traveler are the only pump/filters with a mechanical straining unit and an iodine-impregnated resin matrix, which together effectively disinfect for all enteric pathogens. To boost the taste, the Scout and Explorer can be fitted with a carbon cartridge ($19.95; weighs 3 oz.) that screws onto the bottom of the housing. For the same two models there is also a water bottle adapter ($8.95); it allows you to attach them directly to most wide-mouthed poly bottles. No sanitizing is required before storage or reuse. **PUR Explorer** ($139.95; replacement filter $44.95; weighs 20 oz.; output 3.0 pints/minute; pore size 1.0 microns; capacity up to 500 gallons). This is a larger version of the Scout except for one feature. The Explorer has a self-cleaning internal brush for instant cleaning. Push in the pump handle and give it a quarter turn and a few strokes. **PUR Traveler** ($69.95; replacement filter $29.95; weighs 12 oz.; output 4 oz. with each stroke; pore size 1.0 microns; capacity 100 gallons). The Traveler will disinfect for all enteric pathogens and is suitable for the person staying in hotels where municipal water systems are questionable. The unit is small and quickly produces a glass of treated water, good for brushing your teeth or taking nightly medicines.

The new **PUR *Hiker*** ($44.95; replacement filter $24.95; weighs 11 oz.; output 8.0 pints/minute; pore size 0.5 microns; capacity 200 gallons) is a little different than the other PUR products. It does not contain an iodine matrix and will not eliminate viruses; it has instead a glass-fiber filter that the manufacturer claims has more surface area for trapping particulate matter than most carbon or ceramic filters. Even better, it comes with a one year anti-clog guarantee.

    Pocket *Travel Well* ($29.50; no replacement filter; weighs 2.2 oz.; output 0.25 pints/minute; pore size N/A; capacity 25 gallons; from Outbound, 1580 Zephyr, Hayward, CA 94544, phone 800-866-9880). This is a very small (5.3" x 0.8" diameter)two stage filter/pump with activated carbon cloth and an iodine resin matrix. According to director Ray Higham of Pre-Mac (Kent), Ltd., the British manufacturers of Travel Well, testing has been conducted by some impressive institutions: University of Zimbabwe, London School of Hygiene and Tropical Medicine, British Royal Airforce Institute of Pathology and Tropical Medicine, and Thames Water (specialists in virus testing). Results showed that the activated carbon cloth removed ninety percent of parasitic organisms, even though it was not being relied on for mechanical removal. The iodine had a 99.9 percent kill for protozoa, 99.9999 percent for bacteria, and 99.99 percent for viruses. The Pocket Travel Well is roughly the size of a small tube of toothpaste, though not as heavy — a great system, it would seem, for the marooned hang glider or the ultra-runner. Both Travel Wells are used by the British armed forces as well as the U.N. observers in Cambodia and Mozambique. The housings are made of tough, durable plastic, advertised as being less likely to crack than ceramic and less likely to clog than the small pored filter systems. Both come with an intake hose, a short output hose, and a mesh prefilter for straining out the larger debris. Since the carbon treatment occurs prior to the iodine, the water will taste of iodine. **Trekker *Travel Well*** ($59; replacement filter $32; weighs 5.6 oz.; output 0.5 pints/minute; pore size N/A; capacity 50 gallons). A larger version (5.4" x 1.8")of the Pocket filter/pump.

    PentaPure *Travel Cup* ($15.80; no replacement filter; weighs 4 oz.; output 1.0 pint/minute; pore size N/A; capacity 100 gallons; from WTC Industries, Inc., 14405 21st Ave. N., Minneapolis, MN 55447; phone 800-637-1244). This company supplies PentaPure products to the Peace Corps and U.S. Embassy staffs all over the world. This iodine element works on the same demand-release technology that is used for all the water in the NASA Space Shuttle. Director of sales Ron Moore claims iodinated resin is 100,000 times more powerful than plain iodine. The Travel Cup is a gravity flow system and designed to be discarded after treating one hundred gallons. You can treat water one cup at a time or run it directly into a canteen. The **PentaPure Oasis** ($32, mechanical replacement filter $8.50, iodine replacement filter $12, combined replacement filter $29; weighs 5 oz.; output 2.0 pints/minute; pore size 2.0 microns; capacity 200 gallons) is WTC's new sport model, a squeeze bottle with a capacity of twenty fluid ounces, and a three-stage filter. The mechanical filter (a pleated, porous medium of two microns) takes out protozoan cysts. The iodinated resin kills bacteria and viruses. And activated carbon removes organic chemicals, while improving the taste. **PentaPure Water Jug** ($33; replacement filters same as Oasis; weighs 20 oz.; output 2.0 pints/minute; pore size 2.0 microns; capacity 200 gallons). A collapsible, accordion-style container, the Water Jug is fitted with the same three stage filter cartridge as the Oasis. It will hold one gallon collapsed, two gallons expanded. Set it on a picnic table, open the spigot, and fill your coffee pot. **PentaPure Bucket** ($175; replacement filter $75, weighs 6.6 lbs.; output 10 gallons/hour; pore size 5.0 microns; capacity 1,000 gallons). The five gallon Bucket is a gravity flow system with a two and a half gallon top reservoir, which is filled twice to obtain a whole bucket. The filter cartridge is two stage with iodinated resin and activated carbon. A prefilter removes sediment down to thirty microns. The manufacturers say this model is popular at construction sites and mining camps.

   The Sanitizer ($13; order by mail or fax from Travel and Trail Custom Products, 1430 Willamette, Suite 237, Eugene, OR 97401, fax 503-485-4529) was previously marketed under the name Sierra Water Purifier. It's a quick two-step operation. First, you *super*-chlorinate. Then you add hydrogen peroxide, which combines chemically with the chlorine to form plain H_2O again with a few innocuous salts. Two small bottles capable of treating 160 gallons are compact and lightweight, and the price is right. And it tastes like water! Other pluses: It will disinfect large quantities of water in a hurry and it can be stored in a chlorinated state until ready to use. Chlorides don't present the health hazards known to iodines. I touted this product highly in the first edition of this book and do again, with the caution that *Cryptosporidium* oocysts are highly resistant to any form of chlorine. Until we know more about how super chlorination works, take the added precaution to mechanically prefilter for parasitic organisms. Keep in mind chlorine has a harder time doing its job properly in murky or cold water.

◆

Back in the sixties I often vacationed in Mexico. I remember clutching — with the preoccupation of a small child with a cuddly blanket and separation anxiety — my prescription bottle of tiny lomotil tablets. In those days, lomotil was all that a general practitioner knew to recommend. Today, you can buy Imodium over-the-counter and travel medicine has become a specialty, called *emporiatrics*. A network of travel clinics strung across the country offers informational handouts, provides pre-trip immunizations, suggests appropriate prophylactic medications, and diagnosis post-trip ailments (most people will be home by the time *Giardia* symptoms first appear).

Prophylactic drugs for mild cases of *turista* are generally not recommended for healthy travelers because the medication can get in the way of diagnosis and treatment if you contract something more serious. The exception to this is Pepto-Bismol, which is recommended as both a preventative and a cure. Consult your physician prior to foreign travel about using Pepto-Bismol.

If trekker's trots does get you, it's critical to maintain your hydration. Being unable to do so is considered a medical emergency. Hydration can usually be accomplished orally (provided you're not throwing up) by drinking alternate eight-ounce glasses of:

1. Orange, apple, or any fruit juice rich in potassium with ½ teaspoon of honey or corn syrup with a pinch of salt.

2. Water with ¼ teaspoon of baking soda.

In addition to washing hands and disinfecting water, there are a few easily followed preventive tactics. In developing countries, it helps to stay away from "ground grown" vegetables, especially leafy greens that may have become contaminated by soil, washing water, or unwashed hands. Remember the old adage, "If you can't boil it, cook it, or peel it, forget it!" And don't stuff mid-day traveler's snacks into your mouth with dirty hands. I'm a great one for riding second class buses, running my hands over railings and seat backs and window frames, then at some stop buying a treat from a street vendor — the deliciousness of which is to eat with my fingers while loitering.

Remember all of the above and you can avoid most cases of traveler's diarrhea, as long as you don't stumble out of the jungle into a colorful roadside cafe and order a bottle of pop poured over contaminated ice cubes!

Addresses for other helpful resources follow.

Directory of Clinical Consultants in Tropical Medicine, Medical Parasitology, and Traveler's Health. This is a list of physicians who are members of the American Society of Tropical Medicine and Hygiene. Most are located in the United States; a few are overseas. The directory is offered as a public service and you can obtain one by sending an 8½ by 11 inch SASE with ninety-eight cents U.S. postage to Dr. Leonard Marcus, 148 Highland Avenue, Newton, MA 02165. International travelers are advised to seek medical advice six weeks before departure dates, so plan accordingly.

Center for Disease Control and Prevention, Division of Quarantine, E03 1600 Clifton Road, Atlanta, GA 30333. The CDC is a government agency under the U.S. Department of Health and Human Services. They provide the public with information on endemic diseases, epidemics, and plagues world-wide, with recommendations and requirements for immunizations by country for foreign travel. *Health Information for International Travel,* their yearly publication can be ordered by phone (202-783-3238) with a credit card or by mail from the Superintendent of Documents, U.S. Government Printing Office, Washington, D.C. 20402 (the document number is 01702300192-2 and price $6.50). You can also call the CDC International Travelers Hot Line (404-332-4559), listen to a lengthy message, request faxes, or ask to speak to someone directly. Also available on the hotline is *The Blue Sheet,* a bi-weekly update of the yearly publication. You may be able to avoid a long distance call by first contacting your local county public health department or one of the CDC Public Health Service Quarantine Stations located in Chicago, Los Angeles, Honolulu, Miami, New York, Seattle, or San Francisco.

Health Hints for the Tropics, 11th edition ($5), available from the American Society of Tropical Medicine and Hygiene (ASTMH), 60 Revere Drive, Suite 500, Northbrook, IL 60062. This publication is a bargain basement value for a wealth of information on travel preparation, immunizations, malaria prevention, traveler's diarrhea, and post-trip illness, along with a list of further resources.

The Travel and Tropical Medicine Manual, Elaine C. Jong, M.D. ($34, Philadelphia: W.B. Saunders Company). The first edition is out of print and the price noted here is an estimate by the publishers for the second edition, due out at the end of 1994. This book covers every foreign disease imaginable, if you can struggle through the medical terminology.

The Pocket Doctor: Your Ticket to Good Health While Traveling, Stephen Bezruchka ($4.95, Seattle, WA: The Mountaineers, 1992). A small and more general book for the outdoor addict. It has a good bibliography and a range of odd topics from "hotel fires" to "wild animal attacks" (which to know about might ward off a good case of the shits).

An Explorer's Handbook: An Unconventional Guide for Travelers to Remote Regions, Christina Dodwell (New York: Facts on File, 1986). This one is a favorite of mine for the international bush traveler. With such topics as how to stare down a leopard, how to catch, skin, and cook a crocodile, how to outsmart bush bandits, it is worth reading for pleasure or as an aid to real survival. Out of print, take a trip to the library.

Pecked to Death by Ducks, Tim Cahill ($12, New York: Vintage Books, 1993). Cahill is an inveterate globetrotter with a nose for rare adventure and the pen of a great essayist. This is his latest collection. It will either inspire you to new levels of adventure travel (both high and low) or plant you permanently at home in the rocking chair — a good place to read his other books, *Jaguars Ripped My Flesh* and *A Wolverine is Eating My Leg.*

Infectious Diarrhea from Wilderness and Foreign Travel, an article by Howard Backer, M.D. published in *Management of Wilderness and Environmental Emergencies,* 1994 edition, edited by Auerbach and Geehr (St. Louis, Baltimore, Toronto: C.V.

Mosby). Highly informative, as is the entire book. Find it at your library; the selling price is a whopping $125.

Traveler's Health, How to Stay Healthy All Over the World, Richard Dawood, M.D. ($18, New York: Random House, 1994) was previously published as *How to Stay Healthy Abroad.* This book is a must for travelers wanting to make intelligent decisions about their health, especially when venturing into remote places without physicians or when dealing with language barriers. "There are more physicians in the state of California than in the whole of Africa," Dawood tells us. Written by travelers for travelers, with advice from specialists in every branch of travel medicine. The six hundred pages of practical advice emphasize prevention, with suggestions for cures. This is a fascinating book to read just for the range of bugs that roam the planet — from creepy crawlies to electron-microscopic viruses (E-yi!) — even if you're not planning to meet them all. Invaluable are the fifty pages of appendices, the extensive compilation of travel resources, the geographic distributions of infectious diseases, and the numerous recommendations for further reading. I particularly appreciated the hints for eating under extreme conditions of bad hygiene, when you suspect the dish washing has been unsanitary; they include passing your cutlery through the flame of a candle or a cigarette lighter and leaving the bottom layer of food on your plate. Put down in straightforward (non-medical) English.

1994 International Travel Health Guide, Stuart R. Rose, M.D., ($17.95, Northhampton, MA: Travel Medicine, 1994) is a major reference book, annually updated. Roughly half the book is devoted to "The World Medical Guide" conveniently organized in eleven regions and then by country, giving entry requirements and the telephone numbers of embassies, doctors, hospitals, air ambulance services, and American Express offices. "Disease Risk Summaries" outline what you are likely to encounter in each region. The "Health Advisory" sections give a more local incidence of diseases (country by country) with aspects of transmission, prevention measures, and recommended immunizations. Six hundred traveler's clinics are listed for the United States and Canada.

FOR WOMEN ONLY: HOW NOT TO PEE IN YOUR BOOTS

The significance of my position was the opportunity for my growth.

Valerie Fons, *Keep It Moving*

A chapter for women. Why not? I've been a female all my life, as many a pair of soggy socks, jaundiced sneakers, and rancid leather boots can attest. Men need no pointers on how to pee. Men can pee and maintain the decorum of a three-piece-suiter strolling down Park Avenue. To whizz, men just find a tree. Not to hide behind, thank you, but to lean on while pondering the goings-on of the universe — one hand propped high on the trunk, the other aiming penis. With backs turned but in full view of the world, men piss for anyone present, sometimes in baronial silhouette against a blazing sunset, sometimes without a break in the conversation, as if the flaunting of their ritual were the greater part of its pleasure. Women, on the other hand, search for a place to hide (god forbid anyone should know we have to pee in the first place) where with panties dropped and sweet asses bared, we must assume the position of a flustered duck trying to watch itself pass an egg.

Possibly Freud deserves more credit than I normally grant him. Though I don't recall a childhood Oedipal complex, in adulthood there have been occasions when, along with the urge to pee, I've been seized by a fierce penis envy. But cheer up, my dears, the rest of this chapter is just for us. With a little practice we, too, can cultivate the ultimate in blasé, while being proud of a challenge faced and won, a job well done. (Not just a piddling vaingloriousness in the operation of an appendage come by genetically!)

As a rule, men pee with dignity, it might even be said with class — sometimes with machismo alone, but always with ease. Except when troubled by the inclement conditions reflected in the time-honored proverb, *never into the wind*, men, by and large, are carefree pee-ers. It's high time women peed with a similar sense of pride and had as much fun.

Had I paid more attention when I was growing up in the forties and fifties, my grandmother might well have been my illustrious peeing mentor. Now I have only a remembrance of accompanying her into public restrooms. Hoisting her skirts, she would slip one leg out of her wide-legged underdrawers, twist them around the other leg to hold outstretched matador-fashion, and then with the shuffle of a too tightly reined horse, back bow-legged over the bowl and fire away. In those days, I had no time for this bizarre old-fashioned method: I was too busy balancing little bits of folded paper all around the seat (as my mother had taught me), half of which ended up on the floor from the slight breeze caused by my turning around to sit down. Finding with regularity that a person could water her pants before successfully executing this preparation, I eventually gave it up and just sat down. It was my ignorant but expedient theory that if everyone else were following this ridiculous paper routine, the seat must surely be free from whatever frightful diseases were to be avoided — diseases never explained, only alluded to mysteriously.

To this day, except where sanitary seat tissues ("butt gaskets" in some circles) are furnished for resting upon, I have yet to master a reliable restroom technique. Sometimes I try bracing myself against the stall's walls, toilet tank, or paper dispenser, or even hanging onto the doorknob (if there is one) in an effort to suspend my bum an inch above the seat. About then I remember a couple of friends: one who lets herself in and out of cubicles with a piece of Kleenex and flushes public toilets with her shoe rather than come in skin contact with those germ-ridden levers; the other, a man, who choreographs an elaborate routine for escaping the men's room without touching a thing. Unnerving me further while seated on a sanitary cover is this idle question: If the last person's pee can soak through this thin tissue shield, what else might there be swimming through? Oh, grandmother and baggy underwear, where are you now?

Fortunately, out in the bush we face none of these civilized problems. Give me peeing in the woods any day. Once you get the hang of it, it's a blissful experience. After a long outdoor stint, I find I'm severely depressed with the cold, white, closed-in ambiance and flushing racket of my home bathroom.

In Third World countries, another stand-up peeing style (outshining even my grandmother's) is performed by women who grow up unhampered by underwear. The secret lies somewhere in the tilt of the pelvis and the near bowing of the femurs, which allow peeing with Olympian accuracy. All is made easier by practice since toddler age and the attire of skirts.

Today women think of skirts as less than functional in the woods. The fact that men were originally assigned pants and women skirts was due, in all probability, not to high fashion but to sheer biological practicality.

If you should so desire, don't hesitate to scramble the outbacks in a dirndl or sarong as did Robyn Davidson, the author of *Tracks* (New York: Pantheon Books, 1980), wore crossing the Australian desert with her camels. "Whatever works" is a good philosophy. When we pass on the trail, I'll recognize another independent, experimental spirit. Who can tell? Someday our inhibitions about crotch exposure might evaporate in a revolution similar to "ban the bra" bringing us full circle to the resurrection of the bare-bottomed leopard skin mini! For practical reasons.

I've always said someone could make a fortune designing pants for women with a comfortable velcro-closing crotch. Now the evolution we've all been waiting for has finally arrived. Designer of functional fashion, Vicki Morgan, will surely go down in history with **Zanika Sportswear** (from Outside Interests, Inc., 4315 Oliver Avenue North, Minneapolis, MN 55912, phone 612-521-1429). Uniquely crotch-accessible, Morgan's clothing is for any woman planning to step off the porch — hiker or skier, runner or cyclist, boater or farmer, fisherwoman or cowgirl. Overlapping pull-apart layers in the crotch and front-to-back zippers go beyond any conventional thinking in women's activewear. I can remember trips to the grocery store when I could have used these pants. From bikini briefs, summer shorts, and lycra tights to thermal Long Jaynes, wind pants, and polar fleece jumpsuits, ZANIKA caters to women who pee. I like Morgan's motto: We'll never be caught with our pants down!

It's also possible to master a stand-up peeing technique clothed in a pair of standard loose-fitting shorts — by sliding the crotch material to one side. One friend does this and squats, but another woman I know can adjust the material and then stand right along a roadside to pee. If, in driving by, you miss seeing her stream, you might guess she was only stretching her legs and soaking up the view. Practice is the secret, they say. I am going to practice.

For now, back to wearing shorts, jeans, and bikini underwear, when the process of peeing becomes limited to sitting or squatting. Squatting was never one of my best shots; the liquid soon puddled up and spattered onto everything within three feet. In addition, I have a lousy sense of balance. With all muscles in tight concentration, my success at relaxing the few correct ones to facilitate peeing without toppling over is comparable to my luck on the slot machines: a jackpot once in a lifetime.

Slowly, I recognized that after years of conditioning, I couldn't pee if I couldn't relax, and I couldn't relax if I couldn't sit. So with squatting essentially out of the picture, my experimenting narrowed to various approaches to sitting. In my first attempts, I sat on low rocks. This led again to the puddle-up and spatter effect, the only difference being wet thighs instead of wet ankles.

Then came several tries directly on the ground, based on some left-over-from-college-physics notion that proximity decreases velocity, like pouring lemonade into a pie pan. Direct contact with the earth gave me a primordial closeness to nature but proved disastrous. Either I ended up sitting in the puddle or, trying a slight incline to avoid that, I wound up with a problem rather like trying to anticipate the flow of Kilauea's lava. How far and in which direction was that steaming stuff going to travel? Usually far enough to wipe out the jeans draped around my feet. Furthermore, leaves, burrs, twigs, and foxtails — all having a tendency to stick to my buns — would lodge themselves in my undergarments, ending up in more critical crannies.

A few more days of trial and error dampened yet another theory; sitting on higher objects merely encouraged a more direct route into the boots. But I remained undaunted, enjoying my freedom from walls too much to scurry back to a finely polished, containerized seat, and I set off in search of smoother surfaces away from the spray.

Finally, here it is. For those of us whose squatting muscles have atrophied (a mutation I'm certain paralleled the advent of privy seats), for those of us who didn't grow up on the farm or going fishing with grandpa, and for those of us who wish to experience a piss in the woods with the same high quality of enjoyment one experiences devouring a piece of good New York cheesecake, here is the secret to not peeing in your boots.

First, leave camp in plenty in time to locate an inspiring view, far enough into the bush that your urethra won't tie itself into a bowline at the thought of "being seen." Remember: The can — the only mental relief available on occasion — acquires its reputation for offering restful respite largely because of its isolation. Now look for a spot with two rocks, or two logs, or a rock and a log close together. Slide your pants down around your ankles and seat yourself near the front edge of one rock. Then prop up your feet — off the ground — on the other. Here you can sit, relax, avoid all showers, and keep sticker free. The steep incline of a hillside, the side of a boulder, or a tree trunk can also be used as the second rock. If you're something of a rock climber, you can actually brace yourself in a narrow passageway between two flat-faced boulders or rock walls (a chimney, climbers call it) with your back flat against one side, your knees slightly bent, and your feet flat against the other. In a desert where there are no rocks and logs, you can still sit instead of squat. Pee from the edge of your pack or bedroll; in sand there will be no splatters.

What's more, if you want to coolly flaunt — "this is no sweat for an old hand like me, I was born a frontierswoman" — find a two-rock spot behind a boulder or bush (waist high) from where you can casually, with dignity intact, carry on a conversation with the rest of the camp. Well, maybe not completely intact on the initial try, but be patient. The combination of *women, peeing,* and *dignity* takes a bit of getting used to — not only for you, but for the people with whom you'll be conversing. Be brave. Act "as if" at first; appear nonchalant. Practice. Teach. Be persistent. Eventually the world will change. And in the meantime, keep your feet up and dry while gazing blissfully over the misty mountaintops in complete peace and satisfaction.

◆

The other imperative for women traipsing around in the great outdoors is to engineer a discreet, environmental approach to menstruation. You may never feel as brazen as one woman packer I observed stooped over a campfire cooking breakfast for twenty people. Behind her ear, tucked into her sun-blond curls where one might stick a pencil, she sported a paper-clad tampon, just waiting for a moment's break in the chores. For most of us twentieth-century urban women of propriety traveling in the company of others (and also for any of us who'd rather not offer anyone opportunity to attribute our natural assertiveness to being "on the rag"), here is the plan.

First find a container in which to store your major monthly supply. I've used a regular tin bandage box or a small antique tin. This size works well for applicatorless tampons. A month's supply fits neatly into the small tin, and the tin snugly into the corner of an ammo can, lashed to a raft. When I'm driving horses and my hands stay dirty all day on the trail, I use tampons with applicators. These require a larger container. If you use sanitary pads, you will need one even roomier. The latest designer bag you brought home from boutique shopping, a soft satin travel case, or an old cookie tin all work equally well. This is the main supply and remains stowed away in the depths of your duffel bag or backpack or ammo can.

Now you need a container for daily use — something to keep handy and slip into your pocket when you stroll off in search of your place of easement. A small cosmetic or ditty bag would work, though an ordinary ziplocking bag will do. Inside you will keep a day's supply of whatever you're using, some additional bags for storing refuse (used toilet paper, tampons, sanitary pads, and any paper or cellophane wrappers), and a cache of toilet paper or a pocket pack of tissues. The tissues are a good choice; they can be handed out quite politely to others in need, and the pack can be tucked into a pocket when your day kit becomes jammed. During the day, the refuse bags will reside inside your day kit, stashed in your pocket, a fanny pack, a saddle bag, an ammo can, or an outside pocket of a backpack.

With the new EPA ruling (discussed in Chapter Three), human fecal matter cannot end up in a landfill. Fecally soiled t.p. must be collected, stored, and disposed of separately. It can be burned in your campfire or when you get home in a woodstove; it can be deposited in a Porta Potti or a trailhead vault-type outhouse, or it can be carefully flushed down a toilet connected to a septic or sewer system. A carom effect of the EPA ruling, this is not something that has been well thought out yet. I envision mounds of packed-out toilet paper growing like skyscrapers in community centers. Or we could all learn the water wipe (discussed in Chapter Seven).

The temporary container you use for stashing your soiled tissue should be washable and reusable. A cloth bag of cotton or some space age material seems ideal; it can be thrown into the wash after disposing of the tissue. Perhaps now is the time to break out your Tupperware. Or get busy and craft a poop tube. Or invest in a Go With the J-UGH. Either of the latter you can attach to the outside of a pack and stuff things for days. Otherwise, at evening camp when you resupply your day kit, you will transfer the refuse into a larger holding bag in your main supply bag. If the t.p. transfer process is too distasteful to you, use a fresh cloth bag for each day.

On organized expeditions there is usually a central garbage collection, sometimes sorted into burnable and pack-out types of refuse. To limit the volume and weight of the pack-out garbage, the paper trash is burned in the evening fire or the last thing before breaking camp. Give what you can to the central garbage. Apprise yourself thoroughly of campfire regulations; open fires are not allowed in many areas or may require burn pans and a special ash disposal. Keep in mind also that tampons and sanitary napkins need a hot fire to be completely consumed. Once, when I was a novice in my newly acquired environmental awareness, I returned to camp under cover of darkness and surreptitiously slipped a small carefully wadded bundle into the coals. While we drank Swiss Miss, sang songs, and exchanged flip and wrap stories, to my horror, the fire slowly blackened and peeled away only the wrappings of my gift. The safest thing to do on a group outing is to ask the trip leader or one of the guides about disposal procedures.

After all this, the Enema Man's approach begins to sound pretty good. I can only suggest one thing to help. Think of the days when you're utterly depressed from hearing about desperate situations of people and environments around the world — situations you wish you might change, but there seems to be nothing you can do. Then think about how easy it is — really — to pack out soiled tissue. Our Mother Planet will croon "thank you," and you will know you've actually made a difference for one tiny moment in time. Until it becomes routine, you may have to approach it this way. I do.

◆

Here's a word on feminine funnels: these devices to facilitate a woman's peeing are available in disposal paper or washable, reusable plastic and should by rights be available in every public toilet. The funnel is elongated and elliptical in shape; it affords a comfortable fit between a woman's legs and allows her to direct her stream. It adds a convenient frontal attack to grandmother's stand-up peeing style. I've heard of one woman who carried hers all over Europe and now she's never without it.

Funnels have been used in convalescent hospitals and they are a boon to active women in wheelchairs. I first saw them advertised in *Latitude 38*, a marine publication. They were delighting women sailors who would use them to avoid going below in order to go — a ship's cramped head being the worst spot to hang out if you're prone to seasickness. Using a funnel entailed no dropping of drawers, only an unzipping of shorts or pulling aside of a bathing suit. Women could stand tall — hip to hip with the men — and pee over the rail.

My initial excitement about funnels was in the thought they might be precisely the solution for sleeping out on nippy nights. With a hose, I might pee at 4:00 AM without having to crawl out of a toasty bag. Upon first use, one disadvantage become immediately apparent. The longest of the hoses (and you need the longest in this situation) has a strongly coiled memory. With persistence I could stretch it out, but let go and the end flopped around to spray everything in sight like an out of control fire hose. In addition, if I expected the liquid to exit the correct end, I had to remember the principle of gravity. Having gone to the trouble of hunting up a perfectly flat spot on which to bed, I had to work hard to stay wrapped in the warmth of my bedroll while raising enough to provide a down-hill flow. Though I have reports from women who manage this well, I say forget it! A few moments of scampering about in the frost makes me all the more appreciative of a warm bag. Plus, a daily allotment of minor inconveniences and miseries seems to help me retain a healthy and humble perspective on life.

For anyone interested in experimenting with a funnel, the investment will be small. I've reprinted the name and address of the company that manufactures funnels, because to locate one on hearsay requires the assistance of a well-trained librarian.

Freshette, both plastic and heavy paper models, varied lengths of hose, and collector bags.
> **International Sani-fem Company**
> P.O. Box 4117, Downey, CA 90241
> 310-928-3435 FAX 310-862-4373

In closing this chapter and to warm your hearts, I pass along the following funnel story related to me by an employee of a Sausalito yachting supply house:

> *After carefully selecting a pink plastic funnel, an elderly, white-haired couple arrived at the cash register, whereupon the woman sweetly inquired whether a longer hose might be attached for her. Her request was gladly granted and the funnel whisked away to the back workroom. Then, lifting her gentle, wisdom-aged face toward her husband, with a cherubic wink she crooned, "Now, dear, mine will be longer than yours!"*

WHAT?
NO T.P.?
OR DOING
WITHOUT

Back to the Pleistocene

An *Earth First!* bumpersticker

Conjure up for a moment one of those predawn suburban mornings when you emerge reluctantly from the warm bedding and randomly bump along the walls to the bathroom to sit, just another shadow hunched on the bowl. With eyes shut against the real world, elbows deeply dug into your knees and chin hidden in a cradle of knuckles, you are soon drowsily appreciating the serenity following a particularly portly poop. Then, wishing you could transport yourself back to horizontal and disappear into nothingness again, you blindly grope for the toilet paper only to find your fingertips spinning a naked cylinder of cardboard, sending up the flapping racket of a pinwheel. Rats! You're forced to flip on all one hundred watts, stumble across the room to the cabinet under the sink, and fish out and unwrap a new roll. You might exchange it for the empty one (if you were really a good person), but the dexterity involved would require your final emergence from dreamland.

Or how about this: It's one of those ghastly dinner parties that are not casual and not just old friends. It could be the Waterford and Limoges setting at the elderly boss's estate or maybe the new girlfriend's esteemed literary family all gathered to look you over. The seven-course meal has been consumed, yet the formality of intercourse has not relaxed. As a matter of fact, the guests are perched around the ornate living room like so many stately and stoic great blue herons, picking quietly at thin-layered desserts and sipping tea. Suddenly amidst all this propriety, the spiced prune conserve (which had accompanied the main course and is now somewhere south of your stomach) screams at you to leap up and excuse yourself — politely, of course — on the pretense of helping with the dishes.

Once into the hallway, with pointed toes lifted high in double time, you detour to the bathroom in a perfect imitation of Sylvester the Cat. Shortly thereafter comes the discovery that your hostess has neglected to renew the supply of toilet paper, which — unbeknownst to you — she keeps in the hall closet. You've finished crawling through all the cupboards: now what? Do you hobble to the door with your pants around your knees, poke your nose through the crack, and coolly call, "psst!"? When people disappear into the bathroom at a party, everyone imagines them preening before the mirror, checking for spinach between their teeth, "freshening-up," or possibly tinkling. Straining and pooping? Never. All pretenses go out the window when you holler for toilet paper (in a pinch, women will drip-dry for Number One just like men). For the rest of the evening you may as well wear a sandwich board with three-foot headlines proclaiming what you've been up to.

Next there's the classic Service Station Mad Dash: surely, there isn't a person on the planet who's escaped this one. It begins with the feverish circling of a gas station in an effort to park smack in front of the doors with the stick-figure emblems. Either one that's empty is fair game in emergencies. Somehow you manage to climb out of your vehicle, dance across the pavement in a doubled over version of a cowboy *schottisch* (inspired by constricted sphincter muscles) and throw open the restroom door — oh, miracle of miracles! — without having to humiliate yourself by begging for the key. But there your good fortune ends. Almost immediately you realize the only scraps of toilet paper are flotsam on the lake in which you're standing, there isn't a shred of Kleenex in any of your pockets, and the paper towel dispenser is "god, why me?" empty.

For pure perspective, I recount the above stories or equally painful paperless scenarios for people who respond to the thought of experimenting in the woods without toilet paper as if they'd fallen into a vat of putrefying fish guts! There's nothing so disgusting about it, really.

As with all major changes, adjusting to the absence of that readily available soft and quilted white stuff wound neatly around a cylinder takes a bit of getting used to. Though once successfully maneuvered, brushing one's posterior with a snatch of biodegradable nature can provide a noteworthy experience, whereupon one's ecologically proscribed place in the universe may come vividly into focus. Or even puffed up with ecological pride, or just jubilant with primitive freedom, one might be startled to hear a rousing chorus of approval from the forest fairies. So I've been told.

Doing without t.p. takes me back — way back. Mr. Neanderthal might have had skin like horsehide and needn't have bothered with wiping; but I swear I can sense him and his buddies in their ghostly forms lurking about, curious every time I walk away from a purely organic burial of shit and leaves. After an accomplishment of this sort, I bounce jauntily along absurdly pleased with myself, a euphoric little note within a great harmony. Such mysterious brushes with my deepest origins not only overwhelm but refresh me, as tangibly as a hot shower after a week of mountain sweat and dirt. All at once I feel powerfully attached to a cosmic whole, simple in an age of complexity, perfectly in tune with the world yet tiny and humble and, of all things, enchantingly ancient. Vats of putrefying fish guts — phooey!

Be it a personal quest to function as simply as the primeval wandering tribes, or the thought of not having to pack around rolls of bulky tissue and bags of carry-out garbage — whatever your motivation, here are a few suggestions to get you started. The library is not full of pertinent references to t.p. alternatives, and I will never have covered enough ground to have all the answers. You will have to depart from the text after finishing this chapter and experiment on your own. Call it scientific research.

When I began my evaluation of leaves, I remembered my dear old high school friend who once traveled across Europe keeping a toilet paper diary, replete with sample bits from different countries. She returned to the States with everything from pieces of brown wrapping paper to wax paper and Saran Wrap. Is it, I wonder, worth speculating on the regional correlations between indigenous plant leaves and present day toilet paper quality? If you think you have trouble selecting brands in the supermarket, wait until you see the spectrum nature has to offer.

A vast assortment of leaves, some obviously more appropriate to the task than others, are yours for the picking. But wait. A few words of caution are necessary first:

There are many items suitable for substitute toilet paper, and the choice of living plants should only be a last resort. If you pick leaves at all, be especially mindful. Always select dead grasses and leaves over live ones. Don't pick wildflowers or rare species. Don't pick in parks or other restricted areas. Don't pull anything up by the roots. Don't rob large clumps or strip an entire branch. Carefully pick a leaf here, a leaf there — so no one, not even the plant (especially the plant), will know you have been there. In the following pages you will find many suggestions for nonliving t.p. substitutes.

To hunt leaves, an introductory course in botany is not necessary; neither must you learn every leaf by name. But engrave in your memory poison oak, poison ivy, sumac, and those sneaky stinging nettles, illustrated in any good field guide. A dinner date with Frankenstein's monster or the Wicked Witch of the West would be a joyous interlude compared to the aftermath of using one of those on your keister. If you're seriously planning on hanging around with my Neanderthaloid apparitions and you're also a member of the New Age species I call Exotic Trekkies (those who roam about in exotic climates), I recommend you read up on the vegetation indigenous to the regions you plan to visit, to ascertain whether some peculiar variety of poison pine or viperous honeysuckle ought to be included in your don't-touch list.

Whenever leafstalking, look for the large and the soft. Mullein leaves are my favorite: soft, cushy, almost woolly, and one leaf will do. Thimbleberry is another large-leafed plant and praiseworthy once you discover the soft side opposite the slick. Plants with small or palmated leaves can be used by the handful (remember — one here, one there). Frequently there will be no perfect specimen available. At those times, the profusion and ample diameters of leaves such as California's wild grape may offer compensation for their wax paper slickness.

Before picking, be sure to examine leaves carefully; they sometimes can be sticky (as though covered by a thin layer of syrup), scabrous (having a rasp-like surface), annoyingly prickly owing to small bristles and barbs or, more seriously, hispidulous (covered with sharp hairs stiff enough to penetrate the skin). Stay away from reeds, bamboo, and some grasses — in effect, slicing leaves — that can cause agonizing wounds like paper cuts. With a little care you'll learn which ones to avoid and be on your way to becoming a connoisseur of fine leaves.

Autumn woodlands — not to be shamed by the swankiest powder room decor — offer us a leaf selection in vibrant designer shades. Not all fallen leaves dry and crumble immediately. In some climates, many will stay pliable through the winter months. Alpine winters, where deciduous vegetation is scarce, can be a bit of a problem. For a matter of months in many parts of the high country, evergreens are virtually the only selection. With a little creativity, you can put dried pine needles to good use, provided you have the time to line them all up in the same direction. The odd stick on the ground might be useful, if it's smooth and you remember to rub with the grain. Foresters of the northwest are partial to something I've always known to make great Halloween mustaches — the dark brown *Bryoria* lichen that hangs abundantly from trees in long gauzy streamers. There's also the yellowish green *Alectoria*. And pine cones are reputedly good tools, but steer clear of the spiny rotund cones and stick with the narrower, softer, older sorts. A world-renowned river rafter I know swears by old spongy Douglas fir cones.

My cross-country skiing partner promotes snowballs as the perfect winter wipe — that is, once you brace yourself for the momentary shock. Try it. To me the freeze is a minor trauma compared to visiting one of those portable chemical toilets that sit, invariably in the sun, on construction sites and in campgrounds, exuding breathtaking aromas from the contents cooking within.

Let us return to the glorious woods. In your rummaging in the great outdoors for t.p.-like items, you're bound to find many suitable materials. Try sheets of smooth peeling bark, polished driftwood, seashells, and large feathers. Steer clear of mosses; they're fragile, shouldn't be disturbed, and crumble uselessly anyway.

In the rural areas of many countries, there are people who have never laid eyes on toilet paper. In parts of the Middle East, a person carries a wet cloth into the fields. The custom of religiously eating with the right hand was not born of divine Arab vision but of prudent hygiene: the left hand wiped. I wouldn't want to discourage you if this particular system works for you, but before settling on it permanently, you might consider that for environmental reasons (discussed in Chapter Two) this method will entail carrying along a cloth and two small buckets for rinsing. The second bucket is used to rinse out the first to avoid dipping the fecally contaminated wash bucket directly into wilderness water. Afterwards all wash and rinse water must be buried well away from any watercourse.

There is another paperless technique, but it seldom emerges as an option with our persnickety Western ways, which require by cultural edict keeping copious wads between our fingertips and our bums. This approach comes to us mostly by way of Old World countries and from one well-traveled family physician, Dr. Charles Helm, born in South Africa, now practicing in remote northern British Columbia. We'll call it the *water wipe*.

Nothing is needed but a container for water: a canteen, a cup, a Coke bottle, and a soup bowl have all been suggested. Fill your container and carry it to your chosen spot. Then squatting over your one-sit hole, trickle water from the container into your free hand — never contaminating the fresh water — and there use it to splash or wipe. This trickling procedure poses no problem for agile squatters and good skateboarders, but I find it a difficult maneuver. Almost as efficient as trickling is the repeated moistening of one hand, customarily the left.

The water wipe has its definite pluses. For the minimalist it saves on space and weight — both carry-in and carry-out — and it saves trees (t.p. is not recycled). Unless you're in terrain short on water, the water wipe becomes the ideal wipe. (Tissue can still be carried for instances of traveler's trots.) Don't forget to wash your hands.

Next Dr. Helm takes the whole matter to yet another level by saying if we were to model our diets more after that of horses, we might dispense altogether with wiping, being able ourselves to "neatly pinch off" road apples. A healthy human need not carry *bogroll* (*bog* is a South African euphemism for bathroom) in the wilderness Helm believes, though he admits "the fastidiousness and prudish amongst our number will not be impressed with a blanket ban on bogroll in the bush. . . ."

In a long letter, he goes on:

> *Have you ever watched a horse shit? . . . the process begins with a fart by way of preamble, followed by a voluntary relaxation of the anal sphincter, the passage of a number of well-formed, not-too-hard, not-too-soft turds, then a gentle, well coordinated contraction . . . [whence the whole] falls to the ground without any of its substance remaining adhered to the horse. The entire process is easy, efficient, and above all has no need of toilet paper.*
>
> *Our Western diets have wreaked havoc with our bowel regularity, leading to stools of varying consistency and a consequent increased need for bogroll. We have not only lost the art of shitting in the woods, we have lost the art of shitting, period. Perhaps it is related to the innate fear of being caught with a turd half in and half out, but your average mortal will constrict that sphincter as soon as a respectable fraction has seen the light of day. No turd can withstand this kind of strangulation, and inevitably the distal portion breaks off, the proximal part remains put, and a substantial segment close to the sphincter gets smeared all over. I suspect that most humans tighten that dreaded sphincter half a dozen times per crap. And the bogroll industry gloats and smirks.*

There is definitely something to be said in this regard for a meatless, high fiber diet.

Arid, sandy terrains are the most critically lacking in t.p. substitutes. In a dry creek bed you can sometimes find a smooth sun-baked stone — state of the art wipe! But caution is required. Under a blazing sun, stones can gather enough BTUs to brand cattle. Before using a stone, test it in your hand and then on your wrist as you would milk in a baby bottle. And remember not to return a used stone to the creek bed.

There you have it: all I know today.

Hmm. Well, I once met a man who suggested using sand on my bum in the mountain man's age-old manner of scouring pots and pans. But I have a hunch this curmudgeonly old bugger was, or had, like my own Mr. N., a horsehide ass. I think I'll stick to snowballs and stones.

Now you're on your own.

Definition of Shit

¹**shit**/'shit/*vb.* **shit** *or* **shat** \'shat\; **shit-ting** [alter. (influenced
by ²shit and the past and pp. forms) of earlier *shite*, fr. ME
shiten, fr. OE *-scitan*; akin to MLG & MD *schiten* to defecate, OHG *scizan*, ON *skita* to defecate, OE *sceadan* to divide or separate — more at SHED] *v.i.* 1. to defecate; often
used figuratively to express embarrassment <I thought I'd
~ when I had to pee and there wasn't any place to hide.>
or fear <I just about ~ when I stepped off the ski lift and
viewed the hill from above.>. ~ *v.t.* to defecate something
<~ watery stools>. 2. to fool, to mislead, to put on <You
wouldn't ~ me about using pine cones for toilet paper,
would you?>

shit bricks; 1. to worry. 2. to be terrified.

shit can; 1. to throw away. 2. to ban. 3. to fire or dismiss.

shit fruit salad (also: shit nickels, shit ice cream); said of a
prima donna <she's so special, she must ~>.

shit on; 1. to ruin, to muck up. 2. to treat unfairly, often by
being extremely rude or unkind or harsh.

shit the bed; 1. to foul your nest, to stupidly mess up your
own good situation. 2. to die.

²**shit** \'shit\ *n.* [fr. (assumed) ME, fr. OE *scite* (attested only in
place names); akin to MD *schit*, *schitte* excrement, OE *sci-
tan* to defecate] 1. a: feces b: garbage; junk; unorganized or
unrelated articles, stuff <Never leave ~ in the woods>. 2.
lies, nonsense, exaggeration <a bunch of ~>.

a shit; a derogatory term.

bad shit; a consumable of piss-poor quality; generally refers
to street drugs.

big shit; someone with an overinflated sense of self-impor-
tance.

blow (a person's) shit away; to kill; figuratively, to astound.

built like a brick shit house; well built.

bullshit; 1. lies; nonsense. 2. trash; useless junk. 3. name of
a group word game. 4. an interjection of fierce disagreement.

can eat sawdust and shit 2x4's; 1. is overworked. 2. overly
competant.

*chickenshit; n.*1. a coward. 2. petty behavior. *adj.* cowardly.

crock of shit; something false or deceptive <campaign prom-
ises are usually a ~>.

deep shit; big trouble; also stated *knee deep in shit*.

dipshit; idiot; nerd.

dish out shit; to deliver reprimands or punishments; also, to
abuse verbally.

do bears shit in the woods?; rhetorical reply to statement of
the obvious.

doesn't know shit from Shinola; can't tell the difference
between excrement and brown shoe polish.

dogshit; 1. low-down, dirty, trashed-out. 2. interjection
expressing hot disapproval.

don't give me that shit; 1. shut up. 2. don't kid me.

dumbshit; a pathetic incompetent.

eat shit. 1. to lose a game by a large margin. 2. to get a very
raw deal; to absorb or withstand many insults or even physical abuse. 3. to humble oneself. 4. an angry demand,
meaning to go away, or drop dead.

get your shit together; 1. undergo great personal growth; to
become organized or focused. 2. admonition to hurry up.

give a shit; to care <Mother Nature dear, we do ~>.

good shit; a product of excellent quality or flavor; generally
a reference to street drugs.

Holy shit!; exclamation of surprise, discovery, realization,
or fear.

horseshit; 1. lies, double-talk. 2. interjection of vehement
disagreement.

hot shit; a class act; a popular item; frequently used sarcastically <just because he climbed Everest, he thinks he's ~>.

jack shit; a negative value; to do *jack shit* is to do less than
nothing.

know your shit; to be an expert in your field.

little shit; 1. person of small stature. 2. petty annoyance. 3.
term of endearment for someone who is looked upon
admiringly as a sweet rascal.

No shit!; 1. exclamation ranging from high excitement to
surprise; often similar to Really?; used sarcastically in
response to something already known. 2. exclamation of
hearty agreement.

Oh shit!; exclamation of surprise or disgust; when pronounced \oo shit\ generally a warning of impending
doom; can also mean *Whoops!*; when pronounced

\o sheé it\ indicates great pain or embarrassment, or a colossal disaster; when pronounced \aw shit \ expresses regret or sympathy or shyness.

old shit; things or ideas which have become outmoded; behavior patterns that no longer work; old baggage or agendas.

piece of shit; 1. cheaply constructed article. 2. bad person.

scare the living shit out of; terrorize.

shitburgers; exclamation; an expression of dismay.

shitcan; toilet; garbage can; honey bucket.

shit-eating grin; smile of overt satisfaction.

shit-end of the stick; the rotten part of a deal.

shit happens; expresses the sentiment "the best laid plans often go awry"; often seen on bumper stickers.

shit hits the fan; 1. violent or unpleasant situation, often in reference to reprimands coming down from authority figures. 2. major organizational shake-up.

Shit, man! /shēet män/ 1. generic exclamation for surprise, disgust, delight, anger. 2. expression of pleasure, appreciation, astonishment.

shit on a brick; exclamation of great disgust.

shit on a shingle; creamed chipped beef on toast.

shit on wheels; 1. someone who gets a lot done. 2. a holy terror. 3. a braggart who nevertheless carries it off.

shit or get off the pot; quit wasting time or stalling; make a decision.

shit out of luck; having ill fortune.

stay out of my shit; admonition to mind your own business, to stop meddling.

sure as shit; a very definite and sometimes predictable occurrence; true to form.

take a shit; to defecate.

take shit; to accept abuse or ridicule.

the shits; 1. diarrhea. 2. a dreary, rotten situation; <camping in this cold, damp cave full of bats is ~>.

tough shit; 1. expression indicating bad luck, similar to Too bad! or That's the way the cookie crumbles! 2. angry response, stronger than So what!

up shit creek; in a bad situation.

shitaree *n.* a toilet; Porta Potti; something one shits into.

shit-ass *n.* a reprehensible individual.

shit-bird n. a mild, sometimes half affectionate name for a scoundrel.

shit-brain n. an idiot.

shit disturber n. an instigator.

shit faced adj. drunk or otherwise intoxicated.

shit-fire n. a mean, nasty person; a bully.

shit-fit n. a temper tantrum; a tizzy.

shit-head n. halfway between a shit-ass and a shit-bird.

shit-hole n. 1. a. a toilet b. the hole in the privy board; often used figuratively <financing the research for a biodegradable bag for packing it out would not be throwing money down the ~>. 2. the anus. 3. undesirable place.

shit-house n. 1. a bathroom or outhouse.

in the shit house; in disrepute.

shit house poet; 1. anyone who scribbles graffiti on restroom walls. 2. a lousy poet.

shit list n. a figurative list, implies persons held in low esteem <the person who forgot to pack the toilet paper is on everyone's ~>.

shit load n. big, huge, behemoth.

shit shark n. the person who operates the honey wagon.

shitter n. an outhouse; a toilet.

in the shitter; in disrepute.

shitter time; a place to think things out; discipline in a drug rehab program.

shitty/shit-/ adj., **shit-ti-er**; **-est**. 1. inept. 2. inferior, cheap, bad, or ugly; denotes a state of being that is somehow dreadful, often as a result of physical pain or guilt <my pee ran right down that little mole's hole and now I feel ~>.

Afterword

We need to foster a bosom friendship with land and water and air. I did not once write the word *wilderness* in these pages without some cringing and self-evaluation; I remember the telling words of Chief Luther Standing Bear of the Oglala Sioux:

> We did not think of the great open plains, the beautiful rolling hills, and winding streams with tangled growth, as "wild." Only to the white man was nature a "wilderness" and only to him was the land "infested" with "wild" animals and "savage" people. To us it was tame. Earth was bountiful and we were surrounded with the blessings of the Great Mystery. Not until the hairy man from the east came and with brutal frenzy heaped injustices upon us and the families we loved was it "wild" for us. When the very animals of the forest began fleeing from his approach, then it was that for us the "Wild West" began.

More books from Ten Speed Press

DAYHIKER by Robert S. Wood

Hiking for pleasure and fitness when you don't have the time for serious backpacking. Includes information on equipment and clothing, weight reduction, and fitting a satisfying dayhike into a spare hour or so. $8.95, 128 pages

A WOMAN'S GUIDE TO CYCLING by Susan Weaver

All the cycling basics--buying a bike, road safety, repairs and maintenance, plus in-depth discussion of women's special issues, such as physical fitness and nutrition, cycling during and after pregnancy and with children, and more. $13.95, 256 pages

ANYBODY'S BIKE BOOK by Tom Cuthbertson

A completely revised twentieth-anniversary edition of the classic book for bike owners. Friendly, readable, and clearly illustrated, it shows the do-it-yourselfer how to find the problem fast and fix it. All levels of repairs, for one-speeds through mountain bikes. $9.95, 256 pages

FLATTENED FAUNA by Roger Knutson

The only nature guide that millions of Americans will ever need – a guide to identifying animals once they've been flattened by dozens of vehicles and baked by the sun to an indistinct fur, scale, or feather-covered patty. Was that an old hubcap or a Painted Turtle? A lump of dirt or a yellow-bellied marmot? *Flattened Fauna* provides the answers. $5.95, 96 pages

THE BAREFOOT HIKER by Richard K. Frazine

The title says it all. Here is the unique in outdoor books – all the joys, hazards, myths, and a lot of careful instructions for hitting the trail footloose and sneaker-free. $7.95, 128 pages

WHAT BIRD DID THAT? by Burton Silver & Peter Hansard

Keep this "driver's guide to the birds of North America" in your glove compartment, and you'll never again wonder about who's been decorating your windshield. Full-color illustrations help you identify over 40 of our feathered friends – great fun for kids, ornithologists, and traveling salesmen. $7.95, 64 pages

---

Available from your local bookstore, or order direct from the publisher. Please include $3.50 shipping & handling for the first book, and 50 cents for each additional book. California residents include local sales tax. Write for our free complete catalog of over 500 books, posters, and tapes.

Ten Speed Press
Box 7123
Berkeley, Ca 94707

For VISA, MasterCard, or American Express orders call (800) 841-BOOK.